MURDER
on PERRIN RUN

MURDER
on PERRIN RUN

A Historic Crime in Jefferson County, Ohio

RENA GLOVER GOSS

THE
History
PRESS

Published by The History Press
Charleston, SC
www.historypress.com

Front cover, bottom (*left to right*): *From the* Wheeling Daily Intelligencer, *April 3, 1900*; *from the* Steubenville Herald Star, *October 12, 1900*; *from the* Wheeling Daily Intelligencer, *November 10, 1899.*

Back cover, top (*left to right*): *From the* Steubenville Herald Star, *October 25, 1900*; *from the* Steubenville Herald Star, *October 29, 1900*; *from the* Wheeling Daily Intelligencer, *November 8, 1899.*

Back cover, bottom (*left to right*): *From the* Wheeling Daily Intelligencer, *November 10, 1899*; *from the* Steubenville Herald Star, *October 31, 1900.*

First published 2024

Manufactured in the United States

ISBN 9781467157117

Library of Congress Control Number: 2024938215

Notice: The information in this book is true and complete to the best of our knowledge. It is offered without guarantee on the part of the author or The History Press. The author and The History Press disclaim all liability in connection with the use of this book.

In loving memory of my dear parents, Sterling Joseph Glover and Faye (Grove) Glover, who gave me life, love and a college education.

In loving memory of Larry, my loving and patient late husband who always responded when I called for help with a computer question.

To my dear children, Sarah and Phillip, who, when they were young, thought all families visited cemeteries during their summer vacations.

To my grandchildren, who obediently took the quiz when I asked them to name the ancestors in the framed photographs that hung on the walls of our home.

I love my ancestors, relatives and descendants.

Rena Glover Goss
2024

CONTENTS

Contents

PREFACE

Sterling Glover, my father, and two of his siblings, Harold and Hilda, told stories about their relatives, their ancestors and memories of their childhood near York, Smithfield Township, Jefferson County, Ohio. One of the stories they told frequently originated with their father, William L. Glover. A man named Quincy Cramblett was accused of fatally shooting a local farmer, but it was never proven that Quincy committed the murder. Another story William L. Glover related about Quincy had to do with a dance held at the family home before William L. and his intended wife, Merle Gill, were married in 1903. Quincy asked Merle to dance. She agreed. He said, "I didn't think you'd want to dance with me. I'm Quincy Cramblett." My grandfather William L. Glover promptly asked Quincy to leave.

Before my father's generation died, I entered the stories they told me in a notebook, and that oral history was occasionally consulted while I wrote this book. In the end, the amount of information that my family related about Quincy Cramblett and the crime was correct but minimal. Dad and his siblings never seemed to know anything about the complicated family relationships that unfold in this narrative—or the details about the crime and subsequent trials.

Not everyone is attuned to their family relationships, and certainly, if a shady event existed in a family, it was likely not discussed very much. Young men and women tended to marry who they knew. Many families did not document the vital records of their ancestors or descendants. Marriage license applications didn't originally ask if a couple was related. When the question was finally put on marriage license applications, it asked if the applicants were "closer than first or second cousins," hinting that it was acceptable to marry a relative. Furthermore, a couple may not have known or cared if they were related.

When I first heard the brief outline of the story, I found three newspaper articles about the crime and made copies, which, at the time, were made using glossy black paper with blurry white print and were very hard to read. When copy machines produced better-quality images, I printed a thick notebook full of easy-to-read newspaper articles about the 1899 murder of James H. Gosnell and Quincy Cramblett's alleged connection to the crime.

Newspapers were the media of the day in 1899 and 1900. Daily happenings, local news and world events were presented in newspapers in great detail. The true crime in this story was no different. Reporters for the three Steubenville, Ohio newspapers at the time, the *Herald Star*, the *Weekly Herald* and the *Weekly Gazette*, described this story in extensive and vivid detail. Testimonies in the hearing and two trials let the reader take in the drama about the love, murder and family relationships.

This book was based on the countless articles from the three Steubenville publications. Most of the *Herald Star* articles were accessed online at Ancestry.com, GenealogyBank.com and FamilySearch.org. Since all newspapers have not been digitized and put online, the excellent newspaper microfilm collection at the Schiappa Library in Steubenville was invaluable and provided access to the *Weekly Herald* and the *Weekly Gazette*. Of the three newspapers, the *Herald Star*, founded in 1806, is the lone survivor, published daily in hard copy and online.

Large city newspapers in Cleveland, Pittsburgh and Cincinnati, as well as countless smaller cities, such as Wheeling, Marietta and Cadiz, kept readers informed about the crime and the trials. Denver, Idaho Falls and Lead, South Dakota, plus other cities published regularly about the case. See the bibliography for a more complete list of these publications.

To write this story, I read and transcribed the newspaper articles about the love stories, murder and trials and documented the family relationships through the research of vital records. I contacted descendants of several individuals involved in the story. Many of the descendants had never heard about the love stories, murder or relationships of everyone concerned. After talking with descendants, they showed an eagerness to learn more and offered their encouragement for me to write the story.

Rena Glover Goss
Hudson, Ohio
2024

ACKNOWLEDGEMENTS

I am grateful to the individuals, repositories and online sites that were available to me while I researched this book. Without their availability, this project could not have been completed.

The Jefferson County Courthouse staff was always friendly and helpful in the clerk's office, engineer's office, probate office and recorder's office. They directed and advised me where to search and gladly made copies.

The Genealogy Room in the Schiappa Library at Steubenville always had someone available to help search for information or suggest where to look. Sandy Day, who is now retired, and her successor, Erika Grubbs, could not have done more to help me locate sources and listened eagerly to the story. Newspapers that were not online were available at the library on microfilm.

The Guernsey County Public Library, in Cambridge, Ohio, held some records I needed. Lori recommended sources and directed me to the newspapers available on microfilm.

Foreman James Green at the Northwood Cemetery Office in Cambridge, Ohio, was extremely helpful. After I contacted him with what I needed, he assembled a copy of the records and personally accompanied me to the Cramblett burial plots.

The Historical Society of Mt. Pleasant holds photographs of historical buildings. Pam Dunn graciously retrieved and sent photos of the Odd Fellows Hall, also known as Union Hall, the site of the 1899 hearing.

The Jefferson County Genealogical Society Office holds the original copies of early wills and probate records, plus published books of cemetery, death, birth and marriage records. As a member and volunteer, I had access to these records. Flora VerStraten Merrin, the society's president, was most helpful.

Members of the Harrison County Genealogical Society expressed support of the project. President Susan Adams offered her encouragement and help.

The staff at the Puskarich Library in Cadiz, Ohio, offered encouragement and assistance with the newspapers on microfilm.

The Ohio History Connection in Columbus, Ohio, microfilmed early Ohio newspapers several years ago, which was a tremendous help in my research.

Online sources were most convenient and included: Ancestry.com, FamilySearch.org, GenealogyBank.com and FindaGrave.com.

Several individuals kindly gave me permission to use their records and photographs: Ray and Janet Gosnell of Reynoldsburg, Ohio; Larry E. Gosnell of Texas; and Bob Glover of Cadiz, Ohio.

PART I

LOVE AND MURDER ON PERRIN RUN

1

THE LOVE STORIES

Elva, Cora and Quincy

In 1899, James Gosnell (1842–1899), a farmer, and his wife, Mary Louise (Brown) Gosnell (1855–1930), lived in a primitive clapboard farmhouse on Perrin Run with their two daughters, Elva and Cora. James and Mary Louise moved to their farm about 1875 with their two older children, Charles Clancy Gosnell (1871–1950) and Clara Dell Gosnell (1873–1955).

James Hartley Gosnell, age twenty-eight, married Mary Louise Brown, age fifteen, in Pennsylvania. The age difference of thirteen years was not unusual. Girls often married at a young age, and it was not uncommon for a wife to be as much as two decades younger than her husband.

Located in Smithfield Township, in the southwestern part of Jefferson County, Ohio, the Gosnell farm and home stood in a dark, remote ravine intersected by Perrin Run. The small stream ran from northwest to southeast and emptied into Short Creek near the Long Run Station on the Wheeling and Lake Erie Railway. Short Creek flows into the Ohio River.

Encircled by a picket fence, the Gosnell house sat about two hundred feet back from the "wagon road." In 1899, roads in the area were undeveloped. Travel was done by horseback or horse and buggy on what was referred to as "wagon roads," which were basically just dirt roads. In 1899, telephones and electricity were not common conveniences in Jefferson County farm homes. At that time, such conveniences were either not available or not subscribed to by farm families. In some instances, these conveniences would not appear until the 1940s.

The construction of railroads in the southern part of Jefferson County began as early as the 1850s. To accommodate the emerging coal mining industry, railroad construction greatly increased in the 1870s. By 1899, local passenger train service accommodated smaller villages. Train stops with names but without a station were convenient for persons living in the country. Passengers could board or exit trains at these stops. Two such places were Comly Station and Long Run Station, the closest stops to the Gosnell farm.

Social life for the Gosnell family consisted of church activities, visiting families with whom they were acquainted and helping families who lived on surrounding farms. The Gosnells were church members and regularly attended worship services at the nearby Holmes Methodist Episcopal Church. Two of the Gosnells' daughters, Elva and Cora, attended meetings of the Epworth League, which was a fairly new organization for young people in Methodist churches.

Holmes Methodist Church was established in 1808 near Adena in a beautiful valley on the banks of Short Creek. Frequent flooding eventually washed away the simple structure, as well as some of the grave markers and bodies in the cemetery. About 1810, the church and burial ground were relocated to a higher elevation nearby.

Primitive structures for worship existed at the new location for a few decades until 1874, when, on the spacious and forested higher ground, members constructed a new clapboard church building. In the next few decades, Holmes Methodist Church became a hub for guest preachers and eloquent speakers for Sunday worship and special revivals. Popular social events, such as ice cream eating contests, concerts by the Cadiz Band from Harrison County and Sunday picnic lunches, drew crowds from both Jefferson and Harrison Counties, as well as other communities. Aside from attending the Sunday morning worship services and the social events at Holmes Church, Elva and Cora Gosnell, through their attendance at the Epworth League, became better acquainted with other young people in the community, including Quincy Cramblett.

Quincy Chance Cramblett (1866–1947) lived on a farm about one mile from the Gosnells with his parents, John Cramblett (1836–1910) and Mary Ann (Chance) Cramblett (1831–circa 1918). John Cramblett and Mary Ann Chance were married in 1859. Quincy was the youngest of five children born to the couple. The eldest four children, Mary Josephine, Josiah J., Margaret and Eliza, were married and lived elsewhere. Like the Gosnells, the Crambletts were members of the Holmes Methodist Church. They rented

Holmes Methodist Church, near Adena, was built in 1874 and razed in the 1930s. It was the church the Gosnell and Cramblett families attended. *Bob Glover, photograph collection.*

their farm from Mrs. Cramblett's widowed cousin, Susan (Glover) Comly (1838–1929). Besides providing neighborly help on their respective farms, the Gosnells and Crambletts visited each other occasionally. Mrs. Gosnell was Quincy's first cousin once removed, yet the two families may not have known of their relationship or their common ancestral couple, William and Nancy (Haynes) Barkhurst, who were buried in the Holmes Cemetery.

In 1897, Quincy, aged about twenty-nine, became romantically involved with nineteen-year-old Elva Gosnell. He visited the Gosnell house regularly to see and talk with Elva. At that time, the term *keeping company* meant that when young people were together, they were usually properly chaperoned by family members. Mr. Gosnell, a strict father, permitted Quincy to keep company with his daughter Elva at their home as long as he and the rest of the family were present. *Keeping company* carried with it a stricter set of rules than the later, more progressive practice of dating.

Mr. Gosnell depended on Elva to perform simple chores around the farm. She walked up the hill daily to drive the cattle to the barn or another pasture field. The site of this chore was not visible from the Gosnell home. Quincy often made surprise appearances for a tryst with Elva. She never denied her love for Quincy and confessed that they made love. Whatever tenderness comprised their lovemaking remains a mystery, whether it was kissing, caressing or something more intimate.

Comly house, near Adena. Its owner, Susan (Glover) Comly, rented the property to her cousin Mary (Chance) Cramblett, along with her husband, John, and their family. Tintype, *author's collection.*

By the time the lush green trees of summer faded on the rolling hills to the red and yellow blaze of autumn in 1897, Quincy had proposed marriage to Elva numerous times. Each time, she graciously declined without explanation. Time after time, Quincy persisted with his proposals. Elva vividly remembered the vindictiveness and scorn her father harbored against her older sister Clara and her husband, William Gutshall. Clara married Gutshall against her father's wishes, and James Gosnell never forgave his daughter. Following one of Quincy's many sincere marriage proposals, Elva said, "What if they would use you as they used my brother-in-law?" To which Quincy replied, "That wouldn't hurt you as much as me to do without you."

Still persistent, Quincy continued meeting day after day with Elva at her home and near the pasture field. At their last tryst, Elva boldly proclaimed to Quincy, "We have to quit being together so much." Quincy replied, "I will try. If I can, I will, and if I can't, I will die."

Clara Dell Gosnell was the second child born to James H. and Mary Gosnell. When Clara was twenty years old, she and William Gutshall (1873–

1941) applied for a marriage license in Jefferson County on December 18, 1893. The legal marriage records of that time and place included a "Copy of Marriage Certificate Returned to Probate Judge." The certificate was to be completed by the person officiating at the marriage, but Clara and William's certificate was blank and never completed, which could mean one of several things: (1) no marriage record for the couple appeared in the neighboring counties of Stark and Mahoning, where they lived; (2) the couple could have married in another county or state, and the official failed to complete and file a local certificate; (3) the Jefferson County official who performed the marriage may have failed to complete and file the certificate; (4) or, finally, the couple did not legally marry and only applied for the license. Whatever the reason, Clara entered into the marriage in fervent opposition to her father's wishes. William and Clara Gutshall lived most of their married life in Massillon, Stark County, Ohio. Life was never the same in the Gosnell household afterward. Fear and anger were ever present—fear of who Elva or Cora might marry. Mr. Gosnell became increasingly strict and more irritable with his younger daughters. Plainly stated, life was hell in the Gosnell home.

Families living in rural, sparsely populated areas or small villages associated with and often married someone the family knew whether they were related or not. Intermarriage between relatives in families was commonplace. Family relationships between the Gosnells and the Crambletts were numerous, not to mention complicated. Quincy Cramblett was Mary Louise (Brown) Gosnell's second cousin. Quincy's mother, Mary (Chance) Cramblett, and Mary Louise Brown's mother, Margaret (Barkhurst) Brown (1835–1876), were first cousins.

Mary (Chance) Cramblett's mother, Margaret (Barkhurst) Chance, and Margaret Ann (Barkhurst) Brown's father, Joshua Barkhurst, were siblings. Margaret (Barkhurst) Chance and her brother Joshua were children of William Barkhurst (1785–1861) and Nancy (Haynes) Barkhurst (1784–1842). (See appendix A.)

After Elva declared that she and Quincy had to quit being together so much, Quincy underwent a cooling off period in early 1898. Over the next several months, he spent time reflecting on his tender encounters, emotions and memories with Elva. However, he subconsciously acknowledged that his affair with Elva had ended, never again to be revisited. He hinted to Elva that dying might be necessary if he had to do without her. In the intervening months, Quincy managed to avoid committing suicide. He pondered. He thought. He dreamed.

Suddenly, as if struck by a bolt of lightning, Quincy Cramblett realized that he had never paid any attention to Cora, Elva's younger sister. Sixteen-year-old Cora's dark eyes beamed brightly. She was as beautiful and appealing as any other girl around. Quincy began calling on Cora at the Gosnell home. They also saw each other at Holmes Methodist Church and at Epworth League meetings. For the remainder of 1898, Quincy spent considerable time keeping company with Cora—the family always present, of course. On many occasions, Quincy stayed late into the night, well beyond appropriate calling hours. Knowing that his one-mile horseback ride home would be a dark, tedious trip, Mr. Gosnell, on more than one occasion, invited Quincy to spend the night. Quincy slept with Mr. Gosnell, as was customary in the country for an overnight male guest.

Cora Gosnell, the youngest daughter of James and Mary (Brown) Gosnell and the romantic interest of Quincy Cramblett. *Larry E. Gosnell, Texas, photo collection.*

Winter passed slowly. When the snow melted and the spring of 1899 transitioned to summer, Cora's father became more irritable and impatient with Quincy's constant presence at their home. Mr. Gosnell did not want Quincy coming to the house to keep company with Cora on a daily basis. On more than one occasion, he proclaimed to his wife that the day may come when he would have to hoist Quincy out.

The only reason Mr. Gosnell gave for his disapproval of Quincy was that he did not think Quincy was the right man for Cora. Convinced that no men were worthy of their daughters, many fathers intervened to control their daughters' romantic relationships. On the other hand, Mr. Gosnell regularly invited Quincy back to the Gosnell home, and the two men always appeared cordial to each other. None of the family ever witnessed any exchange of mean, hateful words between the two men. On one occasion, a neighborhood farmer spoke to Mr. Gosnell of Quincy not being too bright, to which Gosnell immediately defended Quincy, accusing anyone who thought that Quincy was not bright of not knowing him.

Mr. Gosnell felt comfortable calling on Quincy for favors. On one occasion, the Gosnell and Cramblett families all attended a social event at Holmes Church. Mr. Gosnell had to return home before dark to do his farm chores. He asked Quincy to bring Mrs. Gosnell, Cora and Elva home after the event concluded. Quincy kindly and graciously drove the women home.

Mrs. Gosnell was uncertain, but she suspected that Cora and Quincy had romantic feelings for each other by the way they acted. She sensed they were keeping company somewhere other than the Gosnell house. She also observed that when Quincy was expected for a visit to the house, Cora would go to the window and anxiously gaze up Perrin Run, waiting for Quincy to come into view.

Like Elva, Cora performed farm chores for her father, such as driving the cattle to the barn or to the other pasture fields. On one hot August day in 1899, Cora went up the hill to drive the cows to the other field. She had lately found herself leaving a little early for the chore, hoping Quincy might appear early as well, which would allow them more time to be together. While Cora waited patiently, she reclined on a green, grassy bank. After watching the fluffy clouds overhead for about half an hour, she jumped with alarm when Quincy bounded down the hill with great excitement and joy. He promptly sat down beside Cora, embraced her tightly, pronounced his love for her and planted a kiss on her waiting lips. Quincy loved Cora passionately and was not bashful about expressing it. Cora always responded in kind with her feelings of love for Quincy.

The summer days shortened, and a cool autumn spread over the trees on the hills with an abundance of flaming color. One lovely Sunday afternoon in October 1899, Quincy and Cora enjoyed a buggy ride that ended at Holmes Church. During the ride, Quincy pressed on with his marriage proposal to Cora. The couple talked in earnest about marriage. Cora shook her head in the negative. Quincy halted the horse near the church. Cora got out of the buggy, walked to the church door, paused briefly and entered. Quincy sat in the buggy for several minutes, gazing at the clear blue sky before finally deciding to drive off toward home.

As late autumn shifted into November, Quincy and Cora continued to meet at the Gosnell home or at their favorite trysting place near the pasture field. Quincy continued to ask, beg and plead with Cora to marry him. He promised that he would take her, do the best for her and care for her as well as anybody else. He promised to get her a ring if she would promise to marry him. Cora could not make the promise. Quincy pressed forward and wanted Cora to promise to marry him sometime in the future. Again, Cora would not make that promise.

Quincy then begged Cora to go with him on Saturday over to Micajah Moore's home to keep company all night. He guaranteed her that no one would ever know. Cora refused to do that because when her folks found out, there would be trouble. Quincy persisted that her folks would never find out. Coge Moore's boy promised it would be alright and that the old folks will never know anything about it. Cora could not be convinced. Quincy resented seeing the girl he loved so much being forcibly held back from him by one man, her father, James Gosnell.

On Monday, October 30, 1899, around 8:00 a.m., when Cora went to drive the cows to the barn, she unexpectedly met Quincy at the cow gap. For a half hour, they carried on a conversation. Quincy continued talking about them getting married, but Cora reiterated that she couldn't marry him now or promise to marry him anytime in the future, especially as long as her father was living. Cora reminded Quincy again of Clara's marriage to Will Gutshall and all the trouble it caused with her father in their home.

She said, "I've seen one racket in the family about marrying and do not want to see any more." Referring to her father, she added, "He don't like Will."

Quincy shot back, "Yes, and I think there's another he don't like."

Cora didn't comprehend and asked, "Who?"

Quincy pointed to himself.

Taken aback by Cora's refusals to his many proposals, Quincy shouted, "Let's kill ourselves and be out of the way!"

Cora, taking her time, was breathless and swallowed hard in disbelief that Quincy suggested such a brazen act. She replied, "I do not want to die that way."

Quincy was insistent and suggested several times that they commit suicide together. Cora refused each time. After the tension eased, Cora mounted her horse and leaned down for Quincy to kiss her goodbye. They rode off solemnly in different directions, each to their respective homes.

2

THE MURDER OF
JAMES H. GOSNELL

Dark fell early on Perrin Run on Saturday, November 4, 1899. The Gosnell family was at home when the clock on the mantel chimed once for 7:30 p.m. After finishing the evening meal, Mr. Gosnell and his daughters Elva and Cora retreated to the sitting room, where he started to read the most recent newspaper. Mrs. Gosnell remained in the kitchen for a short time to seal some jars of apple butter. After she finished that chore, she joined her husband and daughters in the sitting room. Elva moved to the parlor organ and started to play familiar hymns. Annoyed with the loud music, Mr. Gosnell made his way to the kitchen and sat down at the table with his back to the window. He pulled the old oil lamp a little closer so he could see the newspaper print better.

Mrs. Gosnell and her daughters had begun discussing dress fabrics when they were suddenly interrupted by a loud report. Alarmed and thinking that the oil lamp had exploded, they cautiously but quickly made their way to the kitchen and found Mr. Gosnell leaning forward in his chair, holding his chest and moaning. In a matter of seconds, he fell to the floor in dire pain, unable to speak, and then he took his last breath. The women, delirious by now, saw that their father and husband had been shot in his back and that the shot had been fired through the window of their home.

Stunned, the women screamed and immediately feared for their own safety. With no electricity or telephone and hardly knowing what to do next, they quickly pulled down the window blinds, locked the door and rushed upstairs. Through one of the upstairs windows, which they opened, they yelled for help. They did not know what to expect and weren't sure if the shooter still lurked nearby. They did not know if anyone would hear them. All they could think of was their husband and father, who had been shot dead in their own home.

Jeff Rainbow, their nearest neighbor who lived about five hundred yards or a quarter mile up Perrin Run from the Gosnells, was on his way home from Dillonvale at the time. He left the horse trail along Short Creek. As he started up Perrin Run, he paused and thought he heard some wild animals making noises. When he rode farther and listened again, he thought he heard pigs squealing. As Jeff came closer to the Gosnell house, he realized that it was not wild animals nor pigs but women's voices screaming in frantic, tearful, high pitches. Jeff paused on the wagon road, which was about two hundred feet from the Gosnell house. He hesitated momentarily, because he did not know what to do. For around twenty years, Jeff and James Gosnell did not have a friendly, neighborly relationship. Many times in the past, they'd had heated confrontations regarding disagreements over the property lines between their farms. Another time, Mr. Gosnell found some of Jeff's uninvited children in the Gosnell house and ordered them out. When Jeff was younger, Mr. Gosnell had accused him of stealing a watch from the Gosnell house. Another unpleasant argument occurred nine years prior, when Jeff shot the Gosnells' dog. In response to James Gosnell's anger, Jeff threatened to give Gosnell a threshing.

Suddenly, Jeff shifted back to reality mode. He instantly felt compelled to look into the present situation and see why the women were screaming. Jeff dismounted his horse, hitched it to the fence and ran quickly over the short distance from the wagon road to the Gosnell house. The dog barked at him, but he was able to quiet it. He found the women leaning through an upstairs window, sobbing and crying uncontrollably.

With his deep voice, Jeff shouted to them and asked what was wrong. Elva yelled back and told Jeff to come to the door—someone had shot her father. Jeff got to the door and rapped. The panicked, sobbing women came downstairs to meet Jeff and let him in the door. Jeff implored the women to stop screaming and yelling.

The women led Jeff to the kitchen, where Mr. Gosnell lay silent and lifeless in a pool of blood. Shocked by the sight, Jeff paused and then quietly asked what he could do to help. Mrs. Gosnell pleaded for him to go tell her son, Charles, and other nearby neighbors what had happened. Cora asked Jeff to go tell Quincy Cramblett, too.

After the encounter and a brief conversation, Jeff left to perform the favors asked of him. He went to Charles Gosnell's house first and notified him of his father's shooting and death. Jeff next went to notify another nearby neighbor, Clayton Carter (1850–1917). Clayton Carter, Mrs. Gosnell and Quincy Cramblett were second cousins. Clayton's grandfather Isaac Barkhurst (1806–1893), Mrs. Gosnell's grandfather Joshua Barkhurst and Quincy's grandmother Margaret (Barkhurst) Chance were siblings.

Sim Stone, who lived a quarter of a mile from the Gosnells and southeast on Perrin Run, heard the gunshot. David Gotshall, along with his wife and other neighbors Alex and Ella Grimm, heard the screams coming from the Gosnell house. The Gotshalls and Grimms lived on a hill about seven hundred yards west of the Gosnells. These neighbors mounted their horses and rode to the Gosnell house, only to learn that Mr. Gosnell had been shot and was dead.

When Jeff Rainbow notified Charles Gosnell and Clayton Carter, the two men left with Jeff immediately for the Gosnell house. Upon his arrival, Charles Gosnell was overcome at the gruesome sight of his father's cold, lifeless body lying on the floor. He, with the help of Carter and Rainbow, carried Mr. Gosnell's body into the sitting room and placed it on a bed. Jeff returned to his home and brought his mother, Lavina Rainbow, to the Gosnell house to pay her respects to Mrs. Gosnell and her daughters.

After a short time, Jeff took his mother home. During the next two hours, he discussed the shooting with his mother and his wife, Martha (Norris) Rainbow. Jeff's mother said she was reading the newspaper when she heard the gunshot. When she went out on the porch, she fully expected to find that James Gosnell's dog had treed a raccoon and that Gosnell had shot it for his dog. Instead, she heard a scream. She wondered whether it was Cora, because the Rainbow children reported that Cora had been sick at school.

Lavina Rainbow said to her son Jeff that she had heard a horseman gallop by on the wagon road but could not see the rider clearly because of the darkness. She said he seemed to be hooded and covered with dark clothing. He was headed north in the direction of Smithfield.

Lavina Rainbow claimed she heard Quincy ride by so often that she knew the sound of his horse. She believed the horseman to be the shooter and the horseman to be Quincy Cramblett. Jeff harbored misgivings about approaching Quincy Cramblett that night. When the clock struck midnight, Jeff finally decided to ride on and notify Quincy that he was needed at the Gosnell house. Jeff cautiously made his way to the Crambletts' and rapped on the door more than a dozen times before he aroused anyone. Quincy's father, John Cramblett, surprised by the late night caller and groggy from being awakened, made his way to the door. Upon seeing who it was, he asked Jeff what he wanted. Jeff said he was asked to notify Quincy that he was wanted down at the Gosnell house. Jim Gosnell had been shot and was dead.

John Cramblett, taken aback by the shocking news, thanked Jeff and said he would call Quincy immediately. Quincy was asleep upstairs and responded slowly after his father called up the stairway several times. Quincy came downstairs and put on his clothes and boots, which had been left on a chair. He promptly went to the Gosnells' and arrived at about 1:00 a.m.

When Quincy stepped through the kitchen door at the Gosnell house, a tearful Cora came to him quickly, put her arms around him and asked him why he didn't come down last evening. If he had come down, this might not have happened. She quietly led Quincy to the sitting room, and together, they viewed her father's cold, lifeless body. Quincy stayed with the family for the rest of the night and early morning hours.

Sim Stone, the Gotshalls, the Grimms and other folks from the neighborhood who rode by horseback to the Gosnell house tethered their horses wherever it was convenient. Many of these neighbors stayed awake at the house all night, as the custom was not to go to bed and leave the body unattended. Most of those present were reluctant to go back outside the house to bring in drinking water or wood for the fireplace. They feared the shooter was lurking nearby in the dark. Quincy, however, expressed no fear and went outside to get what was needed. The neighbors who were present also noticed that during the long overnight hours, Quincy never inquired about the murder. Everyone at the Gosnell house pondered and discussed who would want to kill Mr. Gosnell. They also wondered what kind of gun the shooter used.

During the late evening and early morning hours, news of James Gosnell's murder spread quickly through the neighboring communities. Hoping to catch the murderer or gather some clues about the crime, dozens of farmers and coal miners who lived near Long Run roamed the countryside. Long Run Station, a stop on the Wheeling Lake Erie Railway, was about three miles from the Gosnell home. Men searched the vicinity all night and into Sunday morning, hoping to discover a clue that would lead to the arrest of the shooter.

On Sunday, November 5, 1899, Quincy helped as needed with farm chores. He rode to Long Run to summon the undertaker and deliver the burial clothes for Mr. Gosnell. Quincy stayed with the Gosnells all day and most of the time until Mr. Gosnell's funeral on Tuesday, November 7.

JAMES H. GOSNELL.

James H. Gosnell. This artist's rendering of the murdered man appeared several times in different newspapers. *From the Lead (SD) Daily Call, "James H. Gosnell," July 18, 1900.*

The village of Mt. Pleasant, located about five miles from the scene of the Gosnell murder, was the closest town from which a phone call could be placed to the Jefferson County sheriff in Steubenville, the county seat. After Sheriff Harry Porter learned of the murder, he and Deputies Stone and Moore made immediate plans to leave Steubenville on the early Sunday morning train. According to a railroad map from the time, the lawmen likely changed trains near or at Warrenton. While the Pennsylvania Railway tracks ran along the west bank of the Ohio River, the Wheeling and Lake Erie Railway ran northwest toward the village of Adena and the coal mining fields. The officers got off the train at Comly Station, another Wheeling and Lake Erie Railway train stop with no station. Comly Station, located about two miles from the scene of the crime, was the closest stop to the Gosnell home. (See appendix B.)

When the officers arrived at the murder scene, they interviewed the Gosnell family members first. Next, they began their search for clues and evidence. One of their initial discoveries revealed that the shooter had rested his gun on a picket fence within five feet of the window through which Mr. Gosnell was shot. The smoke from the gun left black marks on the window sash. Loaded with slugs and wads, the gun pumped four of the slugs into Gosnell's body. The fifth went through the back of the chair on which Mr. Gosnell was sitting. Coroner John A. Fisher, who was on the scene, removed three of the slugs from Gosnell's body. He found a black felt wad outside the window of the Gosnell house. Wads were used in guns to aid in efficiently dislodging the load. Wads, if purchased in a store, were usually made of white felt, but the wads Fisher found were made of black felt.

Foot tracks found near the picket fence appeared to be made by rather small feet and showed that the shooter had on gum boots. Sheriff Porter and his deputies decided that whoever pulled the trigger would likely have received some kind of mark, scratch or injury from the huge load that was discharged from the gun. But in conclusion, the officers did not find enough substantial evidence to make an arrest at that time.

The window in the Gosnell residence through which the assassin fired. In this picture Court Bailiff George Moore is standing in the tracks of the assassin.

"The window in the Gosnell residence through which the assassin fired. In this picture Court Bailiff George Moore is standing in the tracks of the assassin." *From the* Steubenville Herald Star, *"Cramblett," April 2, 1900.*

Theories came forth quickly from residents and the general public about individuals they thought would have a reason to kill James Gosnell. Quincy Cramblett was the first name mentioned for one reason: many neighbors knew of Quincy's romantic involvement with Cora Gosnell and her father's opposition to Quincy. The same people also knew of James Gosnell's stern control of his daughters Elva and Cora. They knew of his vindictive reaction to his elder daughter Clara's marriage to William Gutshall.

In addition, James Gosnell was not on friendly terms with many of his neighbors. Some residents said they knew Gosnell had an unsettled business deal over the sale of a cow to a Frenchman from West Virginia. Gosnell encountered problems when he tried to collect the money from the man. The Frenchman was said to "have it in" for Gosnell. Jeff Rainbow did not escape suspicion. Local residents knew of Rainbow's disagreements with Gosnell about farm boundaries. Gosnell had numerous other confrontations with neighbors on Perrin Run. In the meantime, the public kept busy choosing sides over who they thought committed the crime.

On Sunday, November 5, the day after the murder, Sheriff Harry Porter interviewed Quincy Cramblett, questioning him about his whereabouts on the night of the murder. Quincy assured Porter that he was at home in bed at the time. The sheriff ordered bloodhounds to be brought in from nearby Belmont County to track scents. When the dogs arrived later that day, the tracking around the house lasted only a short time. Quincy Cramblett, calm and composed, showed no fear of the dogs, and the dogs showed no interest in him. The bloodhounds eventually lost whatever scent they had picked up and started tracking sheep.

Following the questioning of the Gosnell family and those present, the sheriff said he needed to search the Cramblett home. Quincy broke down in tears. He had no objection to Sheriff Porter searching, but since John Cramblett, his father, was head of the household, the sheriff would need to get permission to search from Mr. Cramblett. Quincy objected to a search of one room, which contained effects belonging to the owner of the house, Susan (Glover) Comly. John and Mary Ann Cramblett rented the farm and house from Mrs. Cramblett's widowed cousin Susan Comly. Susan stored some of her extra furniture and belongings in a locked room upstairs. Sheriff Porter understood and honored both requests.

Quincy rode along with Sheriff Porter, Deputy Moore and Coroner Fisher to the Cramblett home. John Cramblett gave the officers permission to search his house. During the fifteen-minute search, the officers found a rifle and a revolver. Although Quincy and his father told Porter that they had no shotguns, the officials noticed a bottle half full of shot on the mantel. The men sat down in the living room. Moore leaned his head back against the wall and felt something hard. When he examined a pouch hanging on the wall, Moore discovered a bullet that did not fit either gun in the house. According to Coroner Fisher, the bullet looked and felt about the weight of the slugs found in James Gosnell's body. Through further questioning, the officers learned that Quincy owned a musket, which happened to be missing.

William Cheffy, a neighborhood farmer, had sold a gray horse to Quincy several months before the Gosnell murder. Cheffy met Quincy on the wagon road Sunday morning after the murder. He couldn't help but notice that the left front shoe was missing from Quincy's horse. He warned Quincy about the shoe being off the left front foot of his horse. Quincy informed Cheffy that it had been missing since the previous Saturday night.

Cheffy's wife, Martha A. (Barkhurst) Cheffy, Quincy Cramblett and Mrs. Gosnell were second cousins. Martha's grandfather Jacob Barkhurst; Quincy's grandmother Margaret (Barkhurst) Chance; and Mrs. Gosnell's grandfather Joshua Barkhurst were siblings and children of William and Nancy Haynes Barkhurst.

On Monday, November 6, Sheriff Porter appeared at the Cramblett home and called Quincy outside. Porter greeted Quincy and then informed him that the shoe was off of his horse's left front foot.

Quincy agreed and informed Cheffy that he had lost the horse's shoe the day before while on his way to Long Run, referring to his trip Sunday morning to notify the funeral home about James Gosnell's death. The two stories Quincy told about the horse's missing shoe did not match.

Walter Meek, another local farmer, went to the Gosnell house on Sunday, the day after the murder, and conversed with William Cheffy. Meek and Cheffy walked over the ground where the shooter's horse had allegedly been tied during the murder. They looked only casually at the horse tracks. However, on Monday morning, both men returned and closely scrutinized the horse tracks. They followed the tracks up the road to Jeff Rainbow's barn. The horse tracks showed that the horse had three shoes off and one shoe on. Later that afternoon, Meek and Cheffy examined the feet of Rainbow's horse when it was in the pasture field. They found that Jeff Rainbow's horse had three shoes off and one shoe on. That discovery did not correlate with the "three shoes on and one off" description of Quincy's horse made by other people.

Mr. Gosnell's funeral was held on Tuesday, November 7, at 10:00 a.m., and it brought the entire community together. Gosnell was interred at Holmes Cemetery, which was adjacent to the Holmes Methodist Church, where he and his family worshipped. Grief over his death weighed so heavy on his widow and children that they appeared to be distracted, distant and not themselves.

It appeared that the alleged shooter's horse had been tied to the fence on a narrow strip of ground across Perrin Run that was to the south and out of sight of the Gosnell house. The horse had rubbed its mane and tail against

James H. Gosnell's tombstone in Holmes Pioneer Cemetery, near Adena. His wife, Mary L. (Brown) Gosnell, was interred by his side. *Photograph by the author.*

the fence and left hairs stuck in the wood. The hairs were described as "dirty gray" in color, and the horse tracks were prominent on the soft, moist ground.

Also on Tuesday, November 7, Thomas Marchbank, a neighborhood farmer, stopped to examine the fence where the horse was allegedly tied during the murder. Marchbank mentioned the horse hairs and horse tracks to Coroner Fisher, after which the coroner measured the horse tracks where the horse was allegedly tied.

Later the same day, Quincy came down the road on his horse and tied it in the Gosnell stable. He had come to take care of the Gosnell farm chores. At that time, the coroner took the opportunity to measure the feet on Quincy's horse. More importantly, when Coroner Fisher examined the horse's feet in greater detail, he found that three shoes were on, and one shoe was off. The shoe from the left front foot was missing, and a piece was split out of the inside of the hoof. The right hind foot was worn down in a strange manner. Quincy's horse was a dirty gray color, similar to the mane and tail hairs left on the fence.

After the murder, George F. Gosnell, a nephew of the murdered man, stayed temporarily at the Gosnells' home. The widow Gosnell and her daughters Elva and Cora feared staying alone in the dark, isolated house. They went to live temporarily with Charles Gosnell and his family. George Gosnell's father, Joseph, and the murdered man, James, were brothers.

Two lawmen from Martins Ferry came to the Gosnell house on Tuesday, November 7. They found George Gosnell in charge and asked to talk with Quincy. Since Quincy was at his own home, George volunteered to go to the Crambletts and bring Quincy to the Gosnell house to meet with the officials. George and Quincy talked during the short buggy ride back to the Gosnell house. Quincy wondered if they thought he was a suspect in the murder. George assured Quincy that they might suspect anybody. Quincy felt that if the rest of the family stuck to him, he would be alright. After the Martins Ferry officials questioned Quincy and attempted to gather further evidence, they concluded the evidence they had was still insufficient to make an arrest.

Quincy and George had been good friends for several years. George and Mrs. Gosnell were first cousins. Their mothers, Hannah (Barkhurst) Gosnell and Margaret Ann (Barkhurst) Brown, were sisters. Hannah and Margaret Ann were first cousins to Quincy's mother, Mary Ann, making George and Quincy second cousins. (See appendix A.)

The Jefferson County law enforcement officials initially promised a prompt and speedy arrest of the shooter who killed James Gosnell on Saturday, November 4, 1899. However, their promise did not materialize. On Wednesday, November 8, the Jefferson County commissioners announced a reward in the *Herald Star*, a daily newspaper published in Steubenville. It stated:

> *A reward of ($500) Five Hundred Dollars is hereby offered and will be paid by the Commissioners of Jefferson County, Ohio for the detection, apprehension and conviction of the* **Murderer or Murderers** *of one James H. Gosnell, who was shot at his home in Smithfield Township, Jefferson County, Ohio, on the night of November 4, 1899, said location being two miles north of Long Run station on Wheeling and Lake Erie Railway. T.A. Sharp, C.A. Brown, W.M. Kerr, County Commissioners, Attest: George P. Harden, County Auditor.*

The $500 reward offered by the commissioners energized the residents of Smithfield and Mt. Pleasant Townships to perform their own sleuthing in the hopes of apprehending the murderer, having him tried and convicted and finally claiming the reward.

Constable McMasters proceeded with the active investigation and rode to the Perrin Run neighborhood again on Thursday, November 8. He met with Quincy Cramblett and asked him if he knew suspicion pointed to him as the shooter.

Before Quincy could respond, McMasters continued and informed him that Jeff Rainbow reported seeing a horse that looked like his tied to the fence on Thursday night before the murder. McMasters then pointedly asked first if Quincy had tied his horse to the fence on Thursday before the murder and, second, if his horse was tied to the fence on Saturday, when the murder occurred. Quincy adamantly insisted that his horse might have been there, but he was not.

The same day, November 8, Constable McMasters took Quincy into custody. Together, the men rode to Mt. Pleasant, where Quincy willingly

$500 REWARD.

A reward of ($500) Five Hundred Dol-
lars is hereby offered and will be paid
by the Commissioners of Jefferson
County, Ohio, for the detection, appre-
hension and conviction of the

Murderer or Murderers

of one James H. Gosnell, who was shot
at his home in Smithfield township,
Jefferson, County. Ohio, on the night of
November 4, 1899, said location being
two miles north of Long Run station on
Wheeling & Lake Erie Railway.

T. A. SHARP,
C. A. BROWN,
W. M. KERR.
County Commissioners.

Attest:
GEORGE P. HARDEN,
County Auditor.

"$500 Reward." A newspaper notice that was published numerous times in the *Herald Star* in an attempt to encourage information from the public. *From the* Steubenville Herald Star, *December 1, 1899.*

agreed to be examined by Dr. McGlenn. The doctor examined Quincy's shoulders and could not find any sign of bruising or an injury from a gun's kickback. He did notice a small cut on Quincy's neck, which could have been caused by a percussion cap. Quincy said it had been a pimple. He reiterated that he was at home in bed the night of the murder, which his father had confirmed earlier. Quincy stated that he was never in love with the Gosnell girls and never proposed marriage to either of them. In conclusion, Constable McMasters did not find enough substantial evidence to further detain or arrest Quincy Cramblett.

Theories about the horse tracks abounded and multiplied. Numerous neighborhood residents without the know-how tried to investigate by using unorthodox items to measure the horse tracks. They used sticks and pencils to measure the length of the hoofprints. Because so many neighbors had ridden horses to the Gosnell house the night of the murder, the identification of any one horse's hoofprints with certainty would have been a challenge at best.

While law enforcement officers questioned and investigated, they continuously gathered circumstantial evidence and relied heavily on hearsay. These investigative procedures, the protection of evidence and the training of law enforcement personnel lacked the finesse of advanced late twentieth- and early twenty-first-century investigative techniques, equipment and technology. Twenty-first-century investigative techniques can rely on an individual's cellphone providing their location. Since no one witnessed the shooting of James Gosnell, the searches, questions and answers failed to uncover any substantive clues. In the meantime, Quincy roamed free and did not fail to talk with anyone who asked him questions about the murder or his possible involvement.

The local, regional and national newspapers provided extensive coverage of the crime. The readers were absorbed in the drama. The press rated the love story and murder mystery higher than any spine-tingling stage melodrama, with the acknowledgement that truth is often stranger than fiction. Many citizens searched for clues with less-than-satisfactory results. Readers eagerly pored over the daily and weekly newspaper updates on the case. Residents were determined to find evidence and discover the guilty party. Family members and citizens often fervently disagreed with each other about who committed the murder and frequently ended up on non-speaking terms over the differences of opinion.

3

THE HEARING

Addison C. Lewis, the Jefferson County prosecutor, ordered a hearing in order to formally question Quincy Cramblett and others regarding the murder of James H. Gosnell. Lewis scheduled the hearing for Wednesday, November 22, 1899, in the village of Mt. Pleasant, located at the south end of Jefferson County and five miles from the scene of the crime. The village residents followed the intensive press coverage about the Gosnell murder. They welcomed the hearing, planned to attend and anxiously awaited to hear the story firsthand. Zealous citizens took up a collection to rent Union Hall, also known as the Odd Fellows Hall, for the hearing, as it was a facility that had space to accommodate the anticipated crowd.

Mt. Pleasant's population consisted mainly of families who followed the Quaker faith. The best in each person and charity for all comprises the core of Quaker belief. For example, during the 1800s, when freed or escaped enslaved persons were on their way north, this abolitionist Quaker community offered safe stops in their homes, which were on a route known as the Underground Railroad. Likewise, in this story, the Quaker refusal to believe in the evil of people generated heated discussions between those who believed Quincy Cramblett was innocent of the murder and others who thought he was guilty. Often, these breaches of friendship and family ties likely required long periods to heal.

On November 22, prosecuting attorney Addison C. Lewis, Sheriff Harry Porter, Deputy Sheriff George Moore, Coroner John Fisher, stenographer Campbell and attorney Emmett Erskine traveled to Mt. Pleasant for the

Union Hall/Odd Fellows Hall, Mt. Pleasant, Ohio, the site of the two-day hearing into the murder of James H. Gosnell. *Historical Society of Mt. Pleasant.*

hearing. Erskine was assigned to represent the suspect, Quincy Cramblett. The legal team arrived to find that crowds of people from all over the countryside had trooped into Mt. Pleasant to attend the hearing. Since the murder case was described as one of the most remarkable and mysterious criminal cases in the country, press coverage of the story appeared in multiple cities and states, including Cleveland and Cincinnati, Ohio; Pittsburgh, Pennsylvania; Denver, Colorado; and Wheeling, West Virginia, to name only a few.

When the hearing opened, the large room on the second floor of Union Hall was packed to suffocation with spectators, many of whom were women. The crowd extended down the stairs and into the street. Several people stood on a narrow stone ledge that ran around the building above the first floor. They clung to the open second-story windows, where they could hear what was going on inside.

At 1:23 p.m., Squire Alexander Humphreyville of Mt. Pleasant rapped for order and opened the hearing. Humphreyville and the attorneys, stenographer and officers were seated on the stage. Quincy Cramblett was seated in the center. He was smiling and described as the most composed man in the room. He waved repeatedly to his friends in the crowd. But

PROSECUTING ATTORNEY A. C. LEWIS

Addison C. Lewis, the prosecutor in the first murder trial of Quincy Cramblett. *From the* Steubenville Herald Star, *April 2, 1900.*

as the hearing proceeded, Quincy fixed his eyes on the floor ahead of him. With a visibly trembling hand, he frequently wiped perspiration from his forehead. Since Quincy had not been imprisoned, he was able to walk around town freely and talk to friends and Constable Drake. He ate at the hotel with the attorneys and others who followed the case.

Prosecutor Lewis stated that he was not consulted about the wording in the affidavit and said that whoever wrote the document had committed an error. He asked for the privilege of changing the wording from "shooting with the intent to kill" to "murder in the first degree." Attorney Erskine agreed to the change. Constable Drake signed the document. Quincy Cramblett entered his plea of not guilty.

During the two-day hearing, twenty-four witnesses were called to the stand. On Wednesday, November 22, the first witnesses called were the murdered man's wife, Mary Gosnell; his youngest daughter, Cora; and Coroner Fisher. Mrs. Gosnell appeared weak and unsteady from the events of the past two weeks. Prosecuting Attorney Lewis asked several questions regarding the night of the murder. In her responses, Mary Gosnell explained how she and her daughters heard the shot and went to the kitchen, where they found Mr. Gosnell clutching his chest. And seconds later, he fell to the floor, dead. She said they locked the door, ran upstairs and screamed "Murder!" out an open window. Mrs. Gosnell said they had a dog but that she did not hear it bark and that it usually did not bark at friends. She explained that Jeff Rainbow was the first to come to the house about ten minutes after the shooting. She asked Jeff to notify her son, Charles Gosnell. Cora asked him to notify Quincy Cramblett.

The prosecutor asked Mrs. Gosnell, "Was he, Quincy, paying any attention to either of your daughters?"

Mrs. Gosnell replied, "I never seen any difference between them. He didn't keep company with either of them at the house."

Mrs. Gosnell said her husband did not want Quincy to come to the house to see Cora, as Quincy was not the kind of man Mr. Gosnell wanted

Cora to marry. Mrs. Gosnell said she told her daughter that she thought Quincy was "green."

When Attorney Erskine cross-examined Mrs. Gosnell, he first asked her age. She answered that she was forty-four years old (the reporter thought she looked sixty) and added that she had been married for twenty-nine years. Regarding Cora, she claimed that Quincy Cramblett did not keep company with Cora at the house, but she suspected from their actions toward each other that they were keeping company somewhere. However, in her next statement, she said Quincy had been coming to the house for about two years, which appeared to be the opposite of what she had said in her previous answer. When Quincy visited, she said all of the family was in the room. In her reply to questions about Mr. Gosnell, Mrs. Gosnell said her husband treated Quincy in a friendly manner, but at times, he acted frigidly toward him. She confessed that her husband was "crabbed at times, like most men and hard to get along with."

Erskine asked Mrs. Gosnell about Jeff Rainbow's appearance at the house the night of the murder. She responded and said she showed him Mr. Gosnell's body. Jeff was willing to notify family and neighbors. She said she had known Jeff Rainbow since he was a little boy. He was not on good terms with Mr. Gosnell. She said her husband once accused Jeff of stealing a watch. A few weeks before the murder, when the Gosnell family returned from church, they found two of Jeff's children in the kitchen.

As one child was closing the cupboard door, Mr. Gosnell shouted, "What are you doing here?"

The boy wondered, "Have you seen our turkey anywhere?"

Gosnell sternly ordered them out. "Well, it isn't here. Let me never catch you here again."

Mrs. Gosnell did not know if Jeff had heard this story.

Suddenly raising his hand and pointing to Quincy Cramblett, Erskine asked Mary Gosnell, "Do you believe that boy murdered your husband?"

Prosecutor Lewis objected, and the objection was sustained.

Cora Gosnell was called to the witness stand. The reporter observed that Cora looked ten years older than she had the previous week. Cora stated that she was seventeen years old and had known Quincy for about three years. Over a year previously, Quincy had begun paying attention to her and first proposed marriage. He had proposed many times since then. She testified that on the Monday before the murder, she met Quincy at the cow gap in the fence. He proposed marriage more than once, and she refused each time.

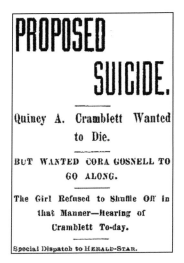

PROPOSED SUICIDE.

Quincy A. Cramblett Wanted to Die.

BUT WANTED CORA GOSNELL TO GO ALONG.

The Girl Refused to Shuffle Off in that Manner—Hearing of Cramblett To-day.

Special Dispatch to HERALD-STAR.

A newspaper headline that appeared in the coverage of the hearing in Mt. Pleasant. *From the* Steubenville Herald Star, *"Proposed Suicide," November 22, 1899.*

She said Quincy seemed frustrated and then shouted, "Let's kill ourselves and be out of the way!"

Cora refused. She did not want to die that way. The suicide-proposal created a sensation and brought forth audible gasps of disbelief from the spectators in Union Hall.

Probing deeper, prosecutor Lewis asked Cora, "You loved him?"

"Yes, sir!" Cora answered promptly and emphatically.

"You told him that?" interrupted Mr. Lewis.

"Yes, sir!" she again replied with emphasis.

Officials did not demand order or make any attempts to restrain the crowd from their uproars of laughter and applause to the testimonies of witnesses or the sarcasm displayed by the attorneys. The Gosnell family members carried in their hearts a grave sense of sorrow from the loss of their husband and father. The raucous discourtesies from the crowd were unbearably painful.

Coroner John A. Fisher testified that he retrieved three bullets from Gosnell's body. He saw the shooter's footprints outside the window. He found the horse's hoofprints matched exactly the hoofprints of Quincy Cramblett's horse. The left front shoe of the horse was missing, and the outside cork on its right hind foot was worn down in a strange manner. Quincy's horse was a dirty gray color, similar to the color of the hairs left on the fence where the alleged killer tied his horse on the night of the murder. Fisher showed one of the horse hairs. He explained many other hairs were there on the fence, but people had carried them away, likely as souvenirs. Sheriff Harry Porter confirmed all of Coroner Fisher's statements about the hoofprints matching the hoofprints of Quincy Cramblett's horse.

Fisher had the bullet that Deputy Moore found at the Cramblett house weighed at the Ridgley Drug Store in Steubenville. The bullet weighed four grains more than each bullet retrieved from Gosnell's body. In conversion from grains to ounces, 4 grains weigh 0.009 ounces.

On Sunday, the day after the murder, Walter Meek and William Cheffy testified that they casually examined the hoofprints of a horse that was in the proximity of the murder scene; they said it had three shoes off and one shoe on. That discovery led them to Jeff Rainbow's barn, where they observed a horse whose hoofs fit that description. The two men returned on Monday and took measurements of the hoofprints where the alleged killer's horse was tied to the fence. Quincy's horse's hoofprints corresponded exactly with their findings. This confusing controversy regarding the different hoof configurations would continue.

Lavina Rainbow, Jeff's mother, testified that she was seventy-four years old and lived with her son and family. On the night of the murder, she said she heard a shot and believed it was James Gosnell shooting a raccoon for his dog. She stepped out on the porch, heard a scream and thought it was the Gosnell girls cutting up. Next, she heard a horse galloping up the road and thought it might be Mr. Gosnell going for the doctor, because she heard Cora had been sick at school. A short time later, Jeff came in and told his mother and wife that James Gosnell had been shot and killed.

Mrs. Rainbow testified further that her son and Mr. Gosnell had not been friends for more than twenty years. Jeff had killed Gosnell's dog. Gosnell had accused Jeff of moving a cornerstone on their property line. Lavina Rainbow did not believe the story about her grandchildren being in the Gosnell house, as they were afraid of Mr. Gosnell. She said there were two old guns at the Rainbow house, but when her husband was alive, there were ten or more guns.

Deputy Sheriff George Moore said in his testimony that he went with Sheriff Porter and Coroner Fisher to search the Cramblett house, where he discovered a bullet in a pouch that was hanging on the wall. He also said he saw a bottle half full of shot on the mantel.

George Gosnell, the murdered man's nephew, testified that he had always been a friend of Quincy Cramblett. He told the court about the visit of Martins Ferry law officials and how he went to Quincy's house to bring him to the Gosnell house for questioning. George told the court about the comment that Quincy made regarding the family sticking with him.

The hearing adjourned late in the day on Wednesday, November 22. When the hearing opened on Thursday, November 23, the first witness called was Robert Chambers, a drugstore owner in Mt. Pleasant. Sometime prior to the hearing, Quincy Cramblett went into the drugstore. Chambers overheard the suspect say that he made gun wads out of an old felt hat.

Dr. McGlenn testified about his physical examination of Cramblett, during which he found no bruises on Quincy's shoulder from firing a gun. He added that Cramblett had a small cut on the side of his neck, which could have been caused by a percussion cap. Cramblett said it had been a pimple.

Constable Stant McMasters, in his testimony, told the court about his conversation with Quincy Cramblett on the Wednesday after the murder. Quincy firmly denied ever being in love with either Elva or Cora Gosnell; he said he never kept company with them and never proposed marriage to either girl.

Attorney Erskine jumped right in with his cross-examination and probed McMasters, "You, an old gray-haired man, inquiring into his love affairs, and he would not tell you?"

McMasters assured Erskine, "I ain't as old as I look."

McMasters claimed that Jeff Rainbow said Quincy's horse was tied near the Gosnell's house on Thursday night before the murder. Quincy held firmly that his horse might have been there, but he wasn't. McMasters added that he had no plans to divide the $500 reward, or blood money.

Early in the investigation, McMasters commented to Will Drake, "D— the blood money."

Drake repeated the statement without the "d—" because he was a Presbyterian, and they don't say such things.

Finally, McMasters testified that he had sworn out a warrant for Cramblett's arrest a few days after the crime and carried it in his pocket but never served the warrant.

Harvey Thompson, George Thompson and Robert Nichols all said that they had been hired by John Cramblett in October 1899 to husk corn. After dinner, the men noticed an old army musket standing in the corner of the Cramblett home. When George picked up the musket, Mr. Cramblett warned him of a possible load in the gun. After George pushed the ramrod down the gun barrel, he estimated that a two-inch load was in the gun.

Jeff Rainbow took the witness stand and said that he left Dillonvale on horseback between 6:30 p.m. and 7:00 p.m. the night of the murder. When he started up Perrin Run, he heard a gunshot and later found the Gosnell women screaming for help out of their upstairs window. Jeff notified the neighbors and Quincy Cramblett. Jeff confirmed that he and James Gosnell were not on terms. About three years prior to the murder, Gosnell's horse had gotten loose and ran away. Jeff caught it, and Gosnell came up the road to get the horse. He looked mad the entire time and never uttered a word, not even a thank-you to Jeff.

Erskine asked Jeff Rainbow why he waited until midnight to notify Quincy Cramblett about the murder. Rainbow responded that his mother heard a horse racing by their house after the shooting and that she had heard Quincy's horse enough to say she believed the rider was Quincy Cramblett. Jeff said he then feared going to the Cramblett house.

Erskine burst forth suddenly, "You didn't shoot Gosnell?"

"No, sir," replied Jeff Rainbow.

Jeff Rainbow confirmed that on the Thursday night before the murder, he saw a red roan horse hitched about five hundred yards below the Gosnell house. He had seen Quincy ride a horse "something like that."

Hugh Best testified that he lived near the mouth of Perrin Run, where it enters Short Creek. While he stood on his porch on that dark night in November, he heard a horse fording the creek. Ten minutes later, he heard the fatal gunshot. Best believed this matched Jeff Rainbow's location when he heard the shot. Best was at the Gosnell home on Sunday morning when he found horse tracks with one shoe missing from the left front hoof. He then measured Quincy Cramblett's horse, and the measurements were exactly the same.

Thomas Scott and Fred Barkhurst testified that they knew nothing about the crime.

Clayton Carter confirmed that on Sunday after the murder, he accompanied Jeff Rainbow to where the horse was allegedly tied. They found no horse tracks, only beaten down grass, as if something had been tramping around on the ground.

James Noble, another witness, said he rode seven miles to the home of Josiah "Si" Cramblett, Quincy's brother, in an attempt to find the missing gun. While Noble was on the witness stand, the prosecuting attorney objected to attorney Erskine's method of cross-examination. The attorneys hurled insults back and forth.

Elva Gosnell, the next witness and daughter of the murdered man, said she was twenty-one years old. She said she had known Quincy Cramblett for three years. He made love to her and asked her to marry him. When Quincy stayed at the house too late, Mr. Gosnell often invited him to spend the night. She added that her father might sometime have to put Quincy out.

David Renner, the last witness, said he had recently been going with Elva. He and Quincy often joked about going to the Gosnell house. Renner stayed overnight on several occasions. He said he never heard Mr. Gosnell speak negatively about Cramblett. Renner said he was present when the bloodhounds were brought to the Gosnell home. Quincy did not exhibit any fear of the dogs. Renner said that one day a few months ago, Quincy asked him if he thought Mr. Gosnell would shoot anyone who ran off with one of the girls. Renner said, "No."

At the conclusion of two days of testimony, two facts remained: no one had witnessed the murder, and all the evidence appeared circumstantial. Defense attorney Erskine made a passionate plea for the release of Quincy Cramblett and rested the case. The spectators applauded.

Demonstrating his dramatic oratory, prosecuting attorney Lewis called attention to the damaging evidence produced by the state in contrast to the defense offering no witnesses to contradict the evidence. Lewis described the motive of and manner of the crime with his florid oratory, after which the hall shook with applause. Squire Humphreyville ordered Quincy Cramblett be held without bond in the Jefferson County Jail in Steubenville until the grand jury could act on the case in January 1900. The *Steubenville Daily Gazette* reported on Friday, November 24, 1899:

> *The Cramblett hearing which was on the boards in the town hall at Mt. Pleasant for two days will go down in history as one of the greatest happenings in the history of the old town. So all could get a chance to hear the testimony a popular subscription was taken up and the hall hired. The people present applauded the tilts between lawyers, and when Erskine went after witnesses with a yell and a grin; or giggled when the love trysts of the Gosnell girls and their fellows were drawn out reluctantly from the young ladies. These doings, which were sacred, were ruthlessly and without compunction dug up and thrown open to public gaze and to serve as manna to gossips.*

4

INDICTMENT, ARRAIGNMENT, TRIAL PREPARATION

The Jefferson County Grand Jury met for seven days and at the conclusion on January 9, 1900, the panel had examined 199 witnesses covering 67 cases. The most important indictment the grand jury returned was against Quincy Cramblett for murder in the first degree. He was charged with shooting James H. Gosnell at the Gosnell home on Perrin Run on Saturday night, November 4, 1899.

On January 17, Clerk Stokes read the indictment to Quincy Cramblett at the Jefferson County Courthouse. The prisoner appeared shabby, unshaven and motionless. He remained silent. Stokes asked Cramblett, "What have you [to] say, are you guilty or not guilty?"

As he dropped his head and looked at the floor, Cramblett replied, "I'm not guilty." He walked to the trial table and signed his name to the plea. He was then arraigned on the charge of murder in the first degree.

Judge Mansfield asked Cramblett if he had counsel, to which the prisoner replied, "No, sir, I have not."

Judge Mansfield appointed attorneys Plummer P. Lewis and Henry Gregg to defend Quincy Cramblett. Mansfield also appointed attorney John M. Cook to assist prosecutor Addison C. Lewis.

Cramblett was taken back to his jail cell. Other prisoners said he acted quite nervous the rest of the day. He paced in and out of the cell until the doors were locked. He experienced a sleepless night in his jail cell.

The prosecutor, defense attorneys and Judge Mansfield quibbled about the trial schedule. The judge proclaimed that cases were usually tried during

A postcard of Jefferson County Courthouse, Steubenville, Ohio, 1910. *www.bing.com/images.*
Public domain.

the court term in which the crime occurred. Prosecutor A.C. Lewis agreed
and moved for the trial to be held in the current term. Defense attorneys
Plummer Lewis and Henry Gregg, being new to the case, pleaded for more
preparation time so they could read the two hundred pages of typewritten
testimony, visit the crime scene and question all witnesses who knew anything
about the case. Judge Mansfield said that since he had appointed skilled and
experienced counsel, he was keeping the trial date of Monday, February 12,
1900, which was about five weeks away.

Defense attorneys Plummer P. Lewis and Henry Gregg prevailed on
Judge Mansfield to eliminate the night sessions of court. They felt the period
between the ending of a night session and the opening session the next
morning did not allow them adequate preparation time. Judge Mansfield
said he would consider the idea, but if one or two more attorneys joined the
request, he would think it was a conspiracy—and he was against conspiracies.

Several things hindered the trial date, originally set for February 12, 1900:
(1) the required time for drawing names from the jury wheel; (2) the sheriff's
schedule to summon prospective jurors; (3) and Judge Mansfield's conflict.
Mansfield had to preside over the court in adjacent Harrison County. By
necessity, the Cramblett trial was moved to Monday, April 2, 1900. This

P. P. LEWIS, ESQ.
One of Cramblett's Attorneys.

HENRY GREGG, ESQ.,
One of the Attorneys for the Defendant.

Left: Plummer P. Lewis, the lead defense attorney in the first-degree murder trial of Quincy Cramblett, April 1900. *From the* Steubenville Herald Star, *"Cramblett," April 2, 1900.*

Right: Henry Gregg, defense attorney for Quincy Cramblett's first-degree murder trial, April 1900. *From the* Steubenville Herald Star, *"Cramblett," April 2, 1900.*

change broke the rule that first-degree murder cases were to be tried in the same court term as the indictment.

In the meantime, Quincy Cramblett was confined to safekeeping with Sheriff Porter in the Jefferson County Jail in Steubenville. During his incarceration, Cramblett found himself a victim of theft. The four dollars in cash and other items that he had in his pockets when he arrived at the jail were placed in an envelope and stored in a safe with the other prisoners' belongings. When Sheriff Porter opened the safe, he found an empty envelope with Quincy's name. Porter concluded that someone had accidentally left the safe open and unattended when the theft occurred.

Before the trial date was set for April 2, 1900, many things had to be accomplished. Witness preparation topped the list, starting with Quincy Cramblett's mother, Mary Ann Cramblett. Mrs. Cramblett was sick and deemed unable to appear in court. Affidavits from Dr. S. Osborne Barkhurst of Smithfield and Dr. John Hanna of Adena were taken and filed with the court regarding Mrs. Cramblett's mental condition.

Dr. Barkhurst said Mrs. Cramblett's first attack of insanity had occurred twelve years prior, in 1888. According to Mrs. Cramblett's birth year of 1831, she would have been about fifty-seven years old at the onset of the first attack of insanity. Barkhurst said he thought "her infirmity was permanent and that she will never be much better." However, Dr. Hanna said in his opinion, "Mrs. Cramblett was only temporarily insane and would be able to testify at the next term of court." Dr. Barkhurst was Mrs. Cramblett's first cousin once removed.

Today, it is common knowledge that early diagnoses of insanity in women were often made at the onset of menopause. In the past, mood swings, depression and unusual behavior, all recognized as symptoms of menopause, typically received a blanket label of "insanity," followed by confinement to a mental institution.

Judge Mansfield ordered the details of the affidavits by the doctors to be kept private and not released to the public. He feared the release could jeopardize securing a jury. The defense attorneys filed a motion asking that a commissioner be appointed to take Mrs. Cramblett's deposition at her home. The motion was granted, and E.S. Pearce was appointed as commissioner to take the deposition. A list of sixty interrogatories regarding Quincy's whereabouts on the night of the murder was attached to the motion.

The investigation about the missing musket continued. When the law officers searched the Cramblett home on November 5, 1899, they found a bullet that did not match any gun in the house. It was allegedly the same size and weight of the bullet that killed James Gosnell.

Quincy later told a friend that he had taken the musket to his brother Si's house two weeks before the Gosnell shooting. Si lived about four miles north of where Quincy and his parents lived. Si Cramblett claimed that he had the musket, but the barn where it was stored had been broken into and the musket stolen.

Harvey Thompson, George Thompson and Robert Nichols worked at the John Cramblett farm two weeks before the Gosnell murder and claimed they saw and handled the musket in the Cramblett home at that time. The musket could have theoretically been stolen from Si Cramblett's barn if it had actually been taken there. Locating the musket was of the utmost importance to the case.

The circumstances surrounding the case continued to engage the public. Three of Steubenville's newspapers, the daily *Herald Star*, the *Weekly Gazette* and the *Weekly Herald*, covered nearly every detail about the love story, the murder, the investigation and the ongoing court proceedings. Regular, if not daily, newspaper coverage of the case occurred in numerous Ohio cities and towns: Cleveland, Cincinnati, Newark, Cadiz, Martins Ferry, Uhrichsville, Marietta, East Liverpool, Delphos, Hillsboro and possibly more. The nearby Pennsylvania cities of Pittsburgh, Indiana and Reynoldsville carried news of the recent events in the case. Newspapers in the more distant states of Colorado, Kansas, Idaho, South Dakota and Nebraska, plus possible others, kept their readers apprised of the most recent news in the case.

PART II

THE FIRST TRIAL

5

JURY SELECTION, TESTIMONY

In preparation for the Quincy Cramblett murder trial, Sheriff Porter and Clerk Stokes drew names of prospective jurors from the jury wheel in mid-March 1900. The sheriff and his deputies served summons to all prospective jurors and to witnesses who were to appear in court. At this time, only men could serve on a jury.

The Quincy Cramblett murder trial opened on Monday, April 2, 1900. The intense examination of nearly seventy men to serve on a jury of twelve required two full days, April 2 and 3. Each man was questioned about the following: if he had formed an opinion about Quincy Cramblett, the accused; if he opposed capital punishment; and if he could render an opinion purely on circumstantial evidence.

Seating the jury of twelve presented a challenge. Many men found they could be promptly excused if they opposed capital punishment, could not render an opinion with only circumstantial evidence, had read newspaper accounts and discussed the case or were sick.

While most men gave brief answers to the questions, some gave unusual responses to questions from the attorneys or judge. Even the attorneys frequently made pointed exchanges with each other.

John Cook, attorney for the state, asked William Wiley of Smithfield what his politics were. Both defense attorneys jumped on that. "We except. This is no political arena. Politics has nothing to do with this." Cook thought politics did have something to do with it and further stated he intended to ask Wiley what his religion was.

William Huston, a prospective juror, presented a certificate issued to him by the City of Steubenville for his service as a volunteer fireman. He claimed the certificate exempted him from jury duty under a law passed thirty-five years ago. He further lectured the judge that the certificate was payment for his service just as a pension was for a soldier. He expounded on the exemptions included in that law. Judge Mansfield thought Huston would make a good juror, as he knew "more law than the court." However, Mansfield excused Huston for other reasons.

Albert McIntyre of Brilliant thought that prisoner Cramblett was innocent. When asked by the prosecutor what his opinion was based on, he replied, "Not guilty." The answer provided a little amusement for the crowd. A few other men claimed to have health issues and hoped to be dismissed. Judge Mansfield dismissed some but seated one who begged not to be seated because of "stomach trouble."

By late afternoon on Tuesday, April 3, 1900, the twelve-man jury had been chosen, sworn in and seated. They were: Jesse Blackledge, Mt. Pleasant; William Wiley, Smithfield; A.O. Davis, Salem; J.B. Lee, Island Creek Township; Harry D. Wintringer, Steubenville; Pierce Carpenter, Warren Township; John Erwin, Steubenville; Stephen Clark, Mingo; Josiah C. Ault, Steubenville; T.C. Weir, Toronto; Wm. H. Cox, Toronto; and David Morrow. The twelve men were kept together during the day in the stenographer's office at the courthouse. The Lacy House, a nearby hotel, provided overnight housing and meals. All of the hotels and boardinghouses in Steubenville were filled with witnesses. Many had to be housed in private homes. The trial was predicted to last ten days to two weeks.

Although it was late on Tuesday afternoon, as soon as the jury was seated, Judge Mansfield called for order. The courtroom was packed with spectators. A great percentage of the crowd were women, who crowded into the front rows, where they could see the handsome prisoner and hear titillating details about Quincy's love affairs with Elva and Cora Gosnell. Attendance increased at every session. Other spectators present acknowledged that this brutal and shocking murder deserved justice for the mourning widow, Mary Gosnell, and her children.

Quincy Cramblett, charged with the first-degree murder of James H. Gosnell, sat beside his defense attorneys, Plummer P. Lewis and Henry Gregg. The accused, thirty-three years old, appeared clean shaven and was dressed in a dark suit with a black necktie. Seated behind the prisoner was his father, John, and his sister and brother-in-law, Mary J. and Addison McClain.

QUINCEY C. CRAMBLETT

An artist's rendering of Quincy Cramblett while he was on trial for murder. The image was published frequently in multiple newspapers. *From the* Steubenville Herald Star, *"Cramblett," April 2, 1900.*

Prosecuting attorney Addison Lewis led with his detailed and descriptive opening statement. James H. Gosnell, he said, was fifty-seven years old and of slight build. Gosnell, his wife and two daughters, Elva and Cora, lived on a farm on Perrin Run in the southwestern part of Jefferson County. Between 7:00 p.m. and 8:00 p.m. on November 4, 1899, Gosnell was shot through the kitchen window of his home while he read a newspaper. His wife and daughters were in another room but rushed into the kitchen to discover their husband and father had been shot. Fearful, screaming and in shock, the women locked the door and rushed upstairs to scream for help.

Jeff Rainbow, the closest neighbor, heard the commotion while he was returning to his nearby home on horseback from Dillonvale. He rode to the Gosnell home and learned of the shooting. Jeff offered his help, and Mrs. Gosnell asked him to notify her son Charles and other neighbors. Cora Gosnell specifically asked Jeff to contact Quincy Cramblett.

Prosecutor Addison Lewis's strategy was to show that the love story, mixed up with the murder, equaled the motive. He stated, "The evidence will show that two years before the murder, Quincy had fallen in love with Elva, the oldest daughter of James Gosnell." Cramblett repeatedly proposed marriage to Elva. Knowing her father's opposition, Elva declined the proposals.

One year later, Cramblett became infatuated with the younger daughter, Cora, aged seventeen. He proposed marriage to her numerous times. Although she professed her love for Cramblett, she declined the marriage proposals, knowing of her father's opposition.

Prosecutor Lewis explained to the jury that Gosnell's eldest daughter, Clara, had married Will Gutshall against Mr. Gosnell's wishes. That event brought trouble to the household and created ill will directed toward Gutshall.

Yet Cramblett made another plea for Cora to meet him at Micajah Moore's house to keep company on the Saturday night one week before the murder. Cora refused. After all of his entreaties had been declined, Quincy said to Cora, "Let us kill ourselves and be out of the way." A gasp went through the courtroom upon hearing the brash suicide proposal.

"The evidence will show," continued the prosecutor, "that once before— or, more often, during the love making—Quincy had proposed the same desperate course."

Lewis proceeded to inform the jury about Quincy Cramblett's behavior when summoned to the Gosnell house the night of the murder. Although Cramblett viewed the dead man's body, he made no inquiries about the details of the murder. He was silent and asked no questions.

The prosecutor said there was a similarity in the weight of a bullet found in the Cramblett home and those retrieved from Gosnell's body. He added that when Cramblett was questioned about the guns he owned, he showed officials a rifle and a pistol. A few days later, he told a friend that his musket had been at his brother's house for four weeks. On October 21, 1899, two weeks before the murder, workers at the John Cramblett farm claimed they saw and examined the musket in the Cramblett home.

Gesturing rhythmically with his index finger to the jury, Lewis said, "The evidence will show that the musket seen in the Cramblett living room on October 21, 1899, will be introduced in evidence here and identified."

The horseshoe configuration and tracks left behind by the shooter's horse where it had allegedly been tied to a fence the night of the murder revealed that it was a horse with three shoes on and an unshod left front hoof. Prosecutor Lewis expounded on several points. "The evidence will show the horse tracks were measured by several witnesses and showed an exact match to Quincy's horse. The evidence will also show that Quincy Cramblett lied. First, Cramblett said he lost the horse's shoe on Sunday morning after the murder, when he went to the undertakers. At another time, Cramblett said he lost the horse's shoe ten days earlier."

Prosecutor Lewis pointed out that after the murder, Quincy Cramblett lied and proclaimed he had no interest in Cora and had never made love to her. Lewis emphasized a conversation between Cramblett and Maggie Best, a young woman in the neighborhood. Maggie told Cramblett he would never get one of the Gosnell girls because their father would not consent. Cramblett allegedly replied, "When I get ready for one of them, I will have her, or either Jim Gosnell or I will be laid in the grave. Jim Gosnell will be no stumbling block to me."

After the lengthy opening statement by the prosecutor, defense attorney Henry Gregg delivered a brief but eloquent and skillfully worded opening statement, calculated to make the jury weigh every point of circumstantial evidence. Gregg gave no hint about what his line of defense would be. His strategy would show that Cramblett was "a farmer's boy, somewhat green, but with conduct that has always been peaceable, quiet, and orderly. His life has been one of kindness and humaneness."

Witnesses were called to the witness stand. They testified under oath and answered questions about the following: Quincy's love affairs with Elva and Cora Gosnell; the controversial identification of the horse tracks made by the alleged shooter's horse; the bullets and wads allegedly used in the shooting; the lies Quincy told; the missing musket; and whether Quincy Cramblett shot crossfire.

Witnesses for the state were called. A.G. White of Toronto, a civil engineer, produced two huge plat maps on a scale of five feet to an inch. Exhibit A showed the layout of the Gosnell home. Exhibit B showed the Gosnell house and its garden, fences, barn and outbuildings, along with Perrin Run, the wagon road and the tree where the murderer's horse was allegedly tied. White spared no details in his long explanation of the maps and drawings. After White answered several questions with more long, detailed answers, the time showed 5:20 p.m. Most of the spectators were gone, but Judge Mansfield continued and called more witnesses.

Dr. S. Osborne Barkhurst testified and said widow Mary Brown Gosnell was his second cousin, which was correct. He knew James H. Gosnell and was summoned to the Gosnell home on Sunday, the day after the murder. He examined Gosnell's body and found five wounds in his back to the right of the spinal column and found five bullets that emerged from the breast while one bullet remained under the skin. Dr. Barkhurst completed the certificate for the coroner. He said he examined the horse tracks, the premises and the black powder marks left on the window sash.

Mrs. Mary Gosnell, the widow of the slain man, was the last witness of the day. She answered questions about herself, her children and the events on the night of the murder as she had told it in the hearing. Her words paralleled what the prosecutor stated regarding Cora and Quincy's relationship, Mr. Gosnell's objections to Quincy Cramblett coming so often to see Cora and Jeff Rainbow's arrival and help on the night of the murder.

Before adjournment, Judge Mansfield instructed the jury that they would be kept together under the control of a special officer, whom they must obey when out of the courtroom. He warned them not to talk about the case with anyone or read Jefferson County newspapers. If a jury member needed to communicate with family, he must notify the court.

Wednesday, April 4, 1900

When the court opened on Wednesday, April 4, 1900, some delay occurred because of the effort to get witnesses into the judge's room. Judge Mansfield instructed the clerk not to pay witnesses who did not report promptly. The judge further instructed Constable Ong to remain at the door and, if a spectator left during the proceedings, not to readmit that person for the rest of the day.

Mrs. Gosnell was recalled to the witness stand and cross-examined by defense attorney Henry Gregg. All of her answers to questions and the statements she made showed how the Gosnell and Cramblett families helped each other with farm work and chores. She spoke of Mr. Gosnell and Quincy trusting each other and said she never heard any unkind words between the two men.

Elva Gosnell, age twenty-two, testified that she had known Quincy Cramblett for about three years. Two years prior, he was a lover of hers and proposed marriage. She knew her father objected, which prompted her to say to Quincy in June 1899, "We have got to quit being together so much."

Quincy told her he would try, but if he couldn't, he would die.

State attorney Cook then probed into Elva's personal space. "What endearing acts did he perform toward you?"

"He kissed me several times," said Elva.

When cross-examined, she explained that Quincy had always acted like a gentleman and said his relations with her father had always been friendly.

Cora Gosnell testified about the Monday before her father was killed. She said she met Quincy near the pasture field. Quincy again asked her to marry him. When she refused, Quincy said, "Let's kill ourselves and be out of the way."

"Did you love him?" asked Mr. Cook.

"Yes, sir," replied Cora emphatically.

"Did he love you?" asked Cook.

"He said he did," said Cora.

When cross-examined, Cora said her father and Quincy were friendly and neighborly. She said she had never heard Quincy say an unkind word about her father or make any threats.

Maggie Best, the young woman who claimed Quincy made a threat against James Gosnell's life, was summoned to testify. However, Maggie's reputation was controversial for several reasons. Maggie Bryant, which was her real name, had been an inmate at the Belmont County Children's

Home. In the past, she had been placed with several families, only to be returned to the home because of her dishonesty. Hugh Best, a neighbor of the Gosnells, took Maggie into his home, a situation that was surrounded by sensational reports. The superintendent and matron of the children's home were present at the court and opposed Maggie taking the witness stand. They were summoned by the defense and planned to impeach any testimony Maggie would give regarding the threat she claimed Quincy made against Mr. Gosnell. Maggie was ultimately not called as a witness.

David Gotshall, his wife, Nancy, and Ella Grimm testified about their quick response to the scene of the murder. J.H. Andrews of the *Herald Star* was called to identify photographs he had taken of the Gosnell house and grounds.

County officials who testified offered surprising and new information derived from their ongoing investigation. John Fisher, a former coroner, displayed an unmerciful sight for the jury to see when he held up the bloodstained garments worn by James Gosnell the night he was murdered. Mrs. Gosnell and her daughters, distraught at the sight, wept and sobbed.

Fisher then produced four bullets that had allegedly pierced Gosnell's body. Fisher had each flattened bullet weighed at Ridgely's Drug Store. The bullets weighed between 39.5 and 47 grains. Converted to ounces, their weights were between 0.09 and 0.11 ounces, respectively. The former coroner described the piece of black felt he found outside the window where the shooting had occurred, the footprints found outside the window and a penholder he found by the window.

The remainder of Fisher's testimony went from the sublime to the ridiculous. The pen was broken off at the end from where it had been caught on the lining of his coat. He put the pen in the cash drawer at his butcher shop, and his son broke the pen while trying to close the drawer. He swore it was the same pen he found in the garden. The prosecutor entered it into evidence, but the defense objected loudly and said it was mutilated beyond reason. The court agreed.

On the night of the James Gosnell murder, the shooter allegedly tied his horse to a fence out of sight from the Gosnell house. After the news of Gosnell's shooting spread, relatives and neighbors rode their horses to the Gosnell house to ask what happened. They then offered to help or assist in whatever way they could. With numerous horses coming from different directions, any reliable evidence about the shooter's horse tracks would be less than creditable.

Fisher, a witness, explained how, with a lead pencil, he measured the horse's hoofprints at the site where the alleged murderer's horse was tied.

When he measured the hoofprints of Quincy Cramblett's horse, they were the same, but he said he lost the pencil.

Sheriff Porter, the next witness, referred to one of the exhibit maps and indicated where he saw a horse had been hitched in a fence corner. The tracks revealed the horse had only three shoes, as its left front hoof was unshod. When the sheriff observed Quincy Cramblett riding his dark gray horse on the road, he could plainly see that Quincy's horse did not have a shoe on its left front hoof.

In cross-examination, defense attorney P.P. Lewis, asked about the numerous horses that were tied to the fence in front of the Gosnell house. Sheriff Porter explained that the horse he referred to was tied 120 yards north of the Gosnell house.

A huge discrepancy arose when Walter Meek, a self-proclaimed horse expert, testified. He concurred that Quincy's horse had three shoes and that its left front hoof was unshod. But when cross-examined, Meek said that while he and Walter Cheffy walked up the road on the Sunday after the murder, Cheffy told him the horse had three shoes off and one hoof shod. They entered Jeff Rainbow's pasture field and found that description fit Jeff's horse.

Sheriff Porter presented nine exhibits, which were pieces and parts of a gun. Some pieces had been found on January 7, 1900, and the other pieces had been found on January 16, 1900, in the woods on Piney Fork Creek, about five miles northwest of the Cramblett home. Porter stated that William Miller had led him to the woods and the places where the pieces and parts of the gun were buried. Miller was married to Margaret Cramblett, Quincy's sister.

Defense attorney Lewis queried Sheriff Porter about expecting the $500 reward. "How much of the reward do you expect to get?…If you secure the conviction of Quincy Cramblett, how much of the $500 do you get?"

Sheriff Porter replied, "I won't get any of it and don't expect any of it."

Lewis asked, "No one is in shape to receive any reward in this case, are they?"

"No, sir," replied the sheriff.

Deputy Sheriff Ross Stone displayed a forty-five-inch-long musket barrel that had been bent in half and shoved down a deep well on Milton Hall's farm near York. Stone spent nearly an hour fishing the barrel out of the well.

Dr. S. Osborne Barkhurst, the next witness, examined the barrel. When asked if he ever owned the gun barrel, he replied, "I wouldn't attempt to qualify as to the gun by the barrel alone. The other parts have much to do with identifying it."

The prosecutor asked, "Did you ever own that gun?"

"I owned a gun exactly like that," replied Barkhurst.

Barkhurst then described the gun he owned and its peculiarities. He said the thumb latch had broken over twenty years ago when the doctor accidentally shot his eye out. He recognized the unusual characteristics and repairs he had made on the parts laid out before him. However, on cross-examination, he said, "Other guns might have some of the same marks."

Hugh Best, the last witness on Wednesday, lived near the junction of Perrin Run and Short Creek, about a mile southeast of the Gosnell home. After hearing about the murder, he went to the Gosnell home and then to Mt. Pleasant to notify the coroner. Best examined the horse tracks and concluded they matched the tracks made by Quincy's horse.

The court adjourned for the day.

Thursday, April 5, 1900

When court reconvened, a large crowd was present. Defense attorney P.P. Lewis entered a complaint about witness James McMannis not remaining in the judge's room. Judge Mansfield ordered the constable to lock the door and said, "If that room ain't big enough to hold him, there is another one that is."

Approximately twenty-two witnesses testified on Thursday. Robert Nichols, George Thompson and Harvey Thompson all testified to seeing and handling the musket at the Cramblett home on October 21, 1899, when they were husking corn for John Cramblett. Nichols noticed that the thumb piece of the hammer had been broken and welded together again. When he was shown the thumb piece that was found in the woods and then entered in the exhibit, he said it looked exactly the same. George Thompson said that on October 21, he picked up the musket and measured the load, which he estimated to be about two inches long.

George Gosnell, a nephew of the murdered man, testified next. George's father, Joseph Gosnell, was the murdered man's brother. George said that four weeks after the murder, he saw a penholder in Quincy's pocket. It matched the penholder the coroner found in the garden outside the window where James Gosnell was shot. When George stayed at the Gosnell house after the murder, two law officials from Martins Ferry came to talk with Quincy. George went to the Cramblett home to get Quincy, and on their return trip, Quincy asked if people suspected him of the murder. George said he didn't know but that they may suspect anyone. Quincy said if the rest of the family stuck to him, he would be all right—and if they didn't, his cake would be dough.

Deputy Sheriff Stant McMasters testified about a conversation he had with Quincy on November 8, 1899, the day after James Gosnell's funeral. "I told him," said McMasters, "that people had measured the horse tracks and they corresponded exactly." Cramblett replied, "Well, my horse may have been there, but I was not."

William Drake testified that he was with the deputy when the conversation with Quincy Cramblett occurred, and he corroborated the deputy's words.

James McMannis's testimony revealed a conversation he had with Cramblett before his arrest but after the Gosnell murder. McMannis encountered Cramblett at the Chamber Brothers' Drug Store in Mt. Pleasant. He asked Cramblett how he loaded his musket to get the shot out successfully.

"I asked him," said McMannis, "if he put in powder, then paper, then shot, then more paper."

Cramblett said, "No, I use wads."

Defense attorney P.P. Lewis asked McMannis, "Can't you testify without so many gyrations of the head?"

The prosecution objected. Judge Mansfield said, "I reserve the right to lecture witnesses, and Mr. McMannis is doing very well."

McMannis continued, and Cramblett said that he cut his wads out of an old hat with a knife instead of a wad cutter.

Hugh Best was recalled for cross-examination by the defense. On the night of Gosnell's murder, Best said he saw Quincy Cramblett helping at the Gosnell home. Cramblett was placing ice about Mr. Gosnell's body and occasionally uncovering the body for visitors to view. Best answered questions about the fence where the shooter's horse was tied. Defense attorney Gregg asked, "Do you know Maggie Best?"

"Yes, sir," replied the witness.

"You are her father, ain't you?" asked defense attorney P.P. Lewis.

The prosecution objected, and the question was ruled out.

Mrs. Lavina Rainbow was the last witness of the morning. She told the court about hearing the shot and the screams and then a horse galloping up the road past her house. She said Jeff went to Dillonvale that day and rode his roan horse. About a half hour after hearing the shot, Jeff came home. She continued, "Gosnell and Jefferson were not good friends and did not speak to each other."

After a lunch break, the court reconvened at 1:30 p.m.

James Noble testified that Quincy told lies and people were catching him in them. He advised Quincy to tell the truth. Quincy insisted he was telling the truth. He said his musket had been at his brother's farm for about a month. Davey Renner was accused of riding Quincy's horse to the Gosnells' the night before the murder. Renner later denied this accusation.

John Ridgley, the drugstore owner, testified about the weight of the bullets. The bullet at the Cramblett house weighed 52 grains. He corroborated the bullet weights taken from Mr. Gosnell's body as given by Coroner Fisher. The prosecutor offered the bullet from the Cramblett house as evidence. But the defense objected. The bullet in a pouch hanging on the wall in the Cramblett house did not show that Quincy had anything to do with the murder. A motion from the defense ordered that Ridgley's testimony concerning the bullet be stricken from the record.

R.A. Linderman, the city marshal of Martins Ferry, and George Campbell, the present coroner, testified that Quincy repeatedly lied and said that he had never been in love with the Gosnell girls and never kept company with them.

William Miller's testimony contained never-before-heard information. Miller, the son-in-law of John Cramblett, and William Noble worked on the Cramblett farm on Monday, November 27, 1899, after the preliminary hearing. After dinner, the men talked with John Cramblett, Quincy's father. Miller and Noble proceeded to the barn and then to the corn crib to search for an old musket. After searching for a short time, Miller found the gun in the corn crib under a mound of ears of corn. He passed it out the door to Milton Hall, who had joined the search. Hall took the musket to the barn, and by the time Miller joined him, Hall had broken the gun up. Hall and Miller bent the gun barrel. Miller identified the gun parts in the exhibit as parts of the gun that belonged to John Cramblett, the same gun which he retrieved from Cramblett's corn crib.

As Miller continued to answer questions, he said he went to the Cramblett house to get a sack for the gun parts. Esther Glover, Mary Cramblett's cousin who was visiting, found a comforter for Miller to wrap around the sack. Upon returning to his own home, Miller burned the wood parts in his stove and took the metal parts to Jim Elliott's woods near Piney Fork, where he buried them. He took the sheriff to the place where the parts were buried.

On December 31, the Sunday after Christmas, Milton Hall removed the gun barrel from the woods. Milton Hall testified that his wife, Margaret

Elizabeth (Glover) Hall, was a cousin of Mrs. Cramblett. The remainder of Hall's testimony about the gun corroborated the testimony of William Miller.

Cook recalled William Miller and asked one question: "Who directed you as to where to look for that gun?" The defense objected, and the objection was sustained.

The state rested its case and retained the privilege of calling on Friday any witness they may have overlooked. The witnesses for the defense were sworn in, and court adjourned until Friday at 9:00 a.m.

FRIDAY, APRIL 6, 1900

On Friday, April 6, 1900, court opened promptly to an ever-growing crowd of spectators. Witnesses were called to the stand soon after the judge's call to order. The state called witness Thomas Marchbank, who lived on Short Creek. He was questioned about the defendant, Quincy Cramblett. Marchbank said that on Sunday, the day after the murder, he encountered Cramblett on horseback near the site where the shooter's horse was allegedly tied. Quincy asked what all the men were doing by the fence. Marchbank said he didn't know. He observed that Quincy's horse did not have a shoe on its left front foot.

Mrs. Gosnell, the widow of the slain man, was recalled. Attorney Cook for the prosecution asked her what relationship existed between her and the defendant, Quincy Cramblett. Referencing hearsay, she claimed she "had heard it said that her grandpap and Quincy's mother's mother were brother and sister." She was correct. Mary Louise (Brown) Gosnell's mother was Margaret Ann (Barkhurst) Brown. Margaret Ann's father was Joshua Barkhurst. Mary Ann (Chance) Cramblett's mother was Margaret (Barkhurst) Chance. Joshua Barkhurst and Margaret (Barkhurst) Chance were brother and sister. So, Quincy Cramblett was a second cousin to Mrs. Gosnell.

Prosecutor Cook recalled William Miller and was determined to get an answer. "Who directed you as to where to look for that gun?" he asked. The defense objected, and the objection was sustained.

He continued, "Who directed you what to do with the gun?" This was objected to, and the objection was sustained. The state then rested its case.

More witnesses were sworn in for the defense.

The first witness called for the defense was Mary Josephine (Cramblett) McClain, the wife of Addison McClain and the sister of Quincy Cramblett. She was first asked to describe the layout of the Cramblett house, and she gave a detailed description of the home. The two-story log house had weatherboarding on the outside with two rooms and a one-story kitchen downstairs. A hallway ran north to south through the house between the two rooms. The sitting room was located to the right of the hall upon entering the house, and that room was used as Mr. and Mrs. Cramblett's sleeping room. A stairway led out of the sitting room to two bedrooms upstairs, one of which Quincy occupied. The stairway was the only access to Quincy's room. Also from the hallway, another stairway led to the second floor, where two locked rooms contained the belongings of Susan (Glover) Comly, the owner of the farm. These two rooms were separated from the other two rooms by a solid plastered partition.

When cross-examined, Mary McLain confirmed a second-floor bedroom was occupied by her brother Quincy. Under the window of Quincy's room, the roof of the kitchen was just a few feet away. The kitchen roof sloped down, and at one corner, a porch rail was also just a few feet away.

In response to questions about her mother, Mary McLain said her mother suffered from mental trouble and had been placed in an asylum thirteen years ago. At present, she concluded that her mother was mentally well but had a physical ailment that prevented her from moving around.

Quincy and Mary McLain's mother, Mary Ann Cramblett, was born around 1831. Thirteen years prior to the trial in 1900, would have been 1887. Mrs. Cramblett would have been about fifty-six, a prime time for menopausal symptoms. This offered a possible explanation for her diagnosis of mental trouble and being placed in an asylum.

Dr. Hanna, the next witness from Adena, confirmed that he was Mary Cramblett's physician. While her health was much improved, he did not think she was able to attend the trial.

Attorney for the defense Henry Gregg then offered the deposition of Mary Cramblett, which was taken at her daughter's home prior to the trial. She gave her age as sixty-nine. On the day Gosnell was killed, she said her husband, John, and Quincy went to Si's farm and returned between 3:00 p.m. and 4:00 p.m. After her husband returned from getting the mail in Adena, the three of them ate supper by lamplight and read their mail. Between 6:00 p.m. and 7:00 p.m., Quincy removed his boots and stockings and went up the stairway from the sitting room. He went to bed in the back bedroom. After her husband locked the doors and covered the fire, they went to bed in the sitting room. Neither of them heard or saw Quincy until he was called for by Jeff Rainbow at midnight. Quincy came down the stairs, put on his boots and left for the Gosnell house.

Dr. Hanna was recalled and said that when he examined Mrs. Cramblett following the November 4 murder, she was insane. However, when he examined her a short time before the deposition, he thought she was sane.

The defense called about thirty-five witnesses to the stand. Each witness was asked their name, occupation and place of residence. All witnesses were asked the question: "Was Quincy Cramblett kind-hearted and humane, peaceable and quiet, and did he have a good reputation?" After each witness gave their name, occupation and residence, twenty-four answered positively that Quincy was kind, peaceable, humane and had a good reputation.

1. A.N. Moore, a former sheriff
2. Charles McKinney, a banker from Smithfield
3. Robert Chambers, the president of the Mt. Pleasant National Bank
4. Joseph Gosnell, the brother of the murdered man
5. William Gosnell, a brother-in-law of the murdered man
6. John Galbraith, the president of the Smithfield Bank
7. Mary Lizzie Comly of Mt. Pleasant
8. David Rennard
9. John Cheffy
10. Charles Gosnell, the son of the murdered man
11. William Carter
12. Mrs. Elizabeth Neel
13. Vernon Young of Long Run
14. Charles Galbraith
15. Mrs. Jeanette Barkhurst
16. Arch Neel Jr., a farmer from Dillonvale
17. John McCabe, a grocer from Dillonvale
18. Edw. S. Smith, a hardware dealer from Adena
19. Ellsworth Barkhurst
20. Montford Moore of Adena
21. B.M. Hastings, a neighbor of the Crambletts
22. Homer Hastings, a neighbor
23. William Rennard, a neighbor
24. Clayton Carter, a neighbor who lived near the Gosnell home

Eleven of the thirty-five witnesses had additional questions to answer or other information to give in their replies.

1. Rev. Peregoy, a Methodist minister from Irondale, was the former pastor at Holmes Methodist Church. He confirmed that Quincy attended church regularly and that the Gosnell girls attended Holmes Church.

2. William Judkins, a Sabbath school superintendent from Smithfield, said Quincy attended the Sunday school class and was as good as any young man he ever knew.

3. Susan (Glover) Comly, who owned the farm where the Crambletts lived, said the Crambletts had moved to the farm three years ago, in November 1897, which was one month after her husband, Wm. Comly, died in October. She said she had been to the farm about six times in those three years and that Quincy had visited her home about three times.

4. Reverend Salmon of Smithfield, who, at the time of James Gosnell's murder, was the pastor at Holmes Methodist Church, said he had known Quincy for nearly two years and had ridden back and forth to church with him. Salmon had never heard anything negative against Quincy in the past.

5. Samuel Vail knew Quincy and never heard a word against him until this charge.

"You never heard that he was arrested before, did you?" asked Prosecutor A.C. Lewis.

"Well, yes, I believe I did hear that." said Vail.

"Did you hear he was in jail?"

"Well, no, sir—I don't remember."

"What was he arrested for?" asked Lewis.

"I heard he was arrested for shooting a squirrel for his sick mother."

The prosecutor revealed that Quincy was arrested on an affidavit filed by Mr. Grafton and fined for shooting squirrels. "Do you know this man Grafton lives in the state of Ohio?" asked Lewis.

"Yes, sir."

"Do you know that Grafton's barn was burned down after the arrest?" asked the prosecutor.

"Yes, sir, I heard it was burned."

"And did you know that they have never yet been able to prove who set it on fire?" asked the prosecutor as the witness was leaving the stand.

6. James Mulholland said Quincy had worked for him.

7. William Hammond of Smithfield was questioned about the burning of the Grafton barn, as was Samuel Vail.

Defense attorney P.P. Lewis interjected that Grafton had Quincy arrested because he shot a squirrel for his sick mother. And he continued, "Where is this man, Grafton? Is he still alive?"

"Yes, sir," Hammond replied

"Is his barn still standing?" asked the prosecutor as the witness was leaving the stand.

8. Lewis Castner attended Holmes Church with Quincy Cramblett.
9. Joseph Kithcart said he had known Quincy Cramblett for thirty years. Kithcart was a school director in the district where the defendant attended school as a boy, and he had a good reputation.
10. Patterson Bell, an engineer who lived on nearby Briar Ridge, had known Quincy for sixteen years. They associated together frequently, and he said that Quincy was a quiet, respectable boy.

When defense attorney P.P. Lewis cross-examined the character witnesses, he aimed to make it appear that Quincy was like other young men: someone who was peaceful, kind and did not engage in fights.

Court adjourned until 1:30 p.m.

11. Oliver Blackburn was the first witness called in the afternoon. A retired merchant from Mt. Pleasant, he had known Quincy for twenty years and said he had met him at Sunday school and church in Dillonvale. He said Quincy was converted during a lengthy meeting at the church about four years prior.

Coroner George Campbell, who acted as the stenographer at the original inquest, answered questions from the defense about Hugh Best's testimony regarding the unshod hoof on Quincy's horse. Campbell was unable to tell if the broken spot on the horse's hoof was on the inside or outside of the hoof.

Clayton Carter, a neighbor of the Crambletts, confirmed that Quincy was a good and kind person. Clayton and Quincy were second cousins. Their mothers, Mary E. (Barkhurst) Carter and Mary Ann (Chance) Cramblett, were first cousins.

The testimony about the missing musket and the uncertainty over the horse's hoofprints were not the only issues that dominated the murder case. A day after the murder of James Gosnell, Deputy Sheriff George Moore examined the ground outside the window where Gosnell had been shot.

Moore found the footprints where the shooter had stood, rested the gun on the fence and fired the fatal shot. While standing in the shooter's footprints, Moore had his photograph taken by the press in a pose that showed the gun had to have rested against the shooter's right shoulder while his left foot was forward, which was a normal position for a person shooting a gun. However, Moore said if a person held the gun against his left shoulder and had his right foot forward, this was known as shooting crossfire The next seven witnesses were questioned about whether Quincy Cramblett fired his gun in a normal position or if he fired crossfire and whether he was right-handed or left-handed at the table or at his work. Harry Paxton, Leander Fulton, George Fulton, Elias W. Fulton, Nathan O. Phipps, William Fisher and Erret Dallas all testified that they had always seen Quincy Cramblett shoot crossfire. A few of the men said that Quincy was right-handed at work or at the table.

During the state's questioning, witnesses Dr. Mercer and George Eberle testified that they saw Jeff Rainbow in Dillonvale at 5:00 p.m. on the afternoon of the shooting. George King said he saw Jeff Rainbow get on his horse at McCabe's store around 6:00 p.m. on the evening of the murder.

Sarah Shively, John Crossley and Clark Thompson testified to the rift between James Gosnell and his neighbor Jeff Rainbow. Shively, a former resident of Perrin Run, said the two men had a dispute over a strip of ground between their farms. She quoted Rainbow as saying, "I guess I will have to kill that s—n of a b—h." The state objected to admitting the testimony because Rainbow's statements could incriminate him. Since Rainbow was not indicted, such statements could not be introduced and were stricken from the record.

John Crossley said bad blood existed between Rainbow and Gosnell. Crossley quoted a threat Rainbow made against Gosnell: "Gosnell and Gotshall have played their hand a long time up that hollow; this thing isn't settled; you mind what I tell you, there will be more than this."

Clark Thompson knew of the difficulties between Rainbow and Gosnell. Thompson heard Rainbow say, "Jim Gosnell won't build any more line fences; it is a long lane that has no turn; you mark what I tell you, and I am damned sure he will never build no more line fences. Gosnell will die with his boots on."

Both sides rested. Court adjourned until 9:00 a.m. on Saturday.

6

ARGUMENTS AND VERDICT

Court reconvened at 9:00 a.m. on Saturday, April 7, 1900. Defense attorneys Henry Gregg and Plummer P. Lewis entered the courtroom first. Attorney John M. Cook for the prosecution entered the room with a flair in his manner of dress. He wore no collar, necktie or vest. Instead, he had a silk kerchief around his neck and a flimsy summer coat. The large crowd of spectators smiled at his appearance, but they really came to hear his eloquent delivery style.

Cook stood quietly with his hands in his pockets when he began his argument for the state. He assured the jury "that in their lives, they had never been called on and they would never be called to perform such a solemn duty as this. Never since Cain slew Abel was there a more horrible crime." Now, with his hands out of his pockets, Cook's voice, accompanied with dramatic gestures, grew louder with every statement he made. He described the stinging murder of James Gosnell and said that, in his judgment, "the State had proven all the links in the chain of evidence against the accused, except one, the threat, and they did not deem it proper to put the witness on the stand." Cook addressed the jury about the law and "reasonable doubt." Furthermore, he pronounced, "You can only prove great crimes like this by circumstantial evidence."

More than once, he thrust his index finger close to Quincy's face and accused him of knowing about the crime that dark night at the Gosnell house. "Cramblett, you needed no telling about the crime; you knew." Whirling about, Cook grew tragic and moved in close to the jurors. He looked the jury members in their eyes and pointed his index finger close to their faces. He said they knew the gun in evidence was the one that killed Gosnell. He emphasized the lies Quincy told, the alibi Quincy's mother gave and the fact that Quincy's father, John Cramblett, did not testify. Good character won't stand up. Quincy Cramblett took precaution that night by not shooting crossfire.

Cook expounded about Quincy's lies to the officers when they searched the Cramblett home. Quincy showed only the two guns that were in the house. "Where is Si Cramblett, Quincy's brother, who allegedly had the musket at his house?" Cook mused. He said the musket never was at Si's house—Quincy lied. The musket was then hidden in John Cramblett's corn crib, retrieved and broken apart by relatives. Blood was thicker than water. Why was it all so secret? "John Cramblett, stand up and tell why this was done."

Cook continued, "Quincy, your horse was down on the strip of ground near Gosnells, and you were there on that Saturday night! All things indicated that the horse was there. I say there were three shod feet and one unshod." No other horse in the community had the same tracks as Quincy's horse. Cook concluded, "The circumstances show that Cramblett is guilty." Cook urged the jury to find a verdict of guilty. The press credited Cook's argument as "able, strong and eloquent."

Defense attorney Plummer P. Lewis's stirring oratory reminded the jury that "the indictment is not an evidence of defendant's guilt" and "that motive does not prove crime." Cramblett and Gosnell were kind to each other. Cramblett did everything he was asked to do during the investigation. Lewis reminded the jurors that they must be satisfied beyond a reasonable doubt that Cramblett killed Gosnell before finding a guilty verdict. "Witnesses," he said, "told different stories about the horse's shoes." He warned that the horse tracks attributed to Quincy's horse were not reliable and should not be considered. One set of horse tracks were traced to Jeff Rainbow's barn. At that point, the judge declared a recess for lunch until 1:00 p.m.

When court reconvened in the afternoon, defense attorney P.P. Lewis continued with his argument. He asked, "Where is Jeff Rainbow, who said he would kill Gosnell some day?…The man who was in a feud of twenty years with Gosnell. The line fence, the stolen watch tell who had a grudge against Gosnell." Many innocent people have been convicted on circumstantial evidence. Lewis concluded his argument and urged the jury to rely on facts, not suspicion. Lewis's plea of innocence for the defendant was intense and eloquent.

Defense attorney Henry Gregg spoke next. He said that when the crime was committed, officers looked to Jeff Rainbow for evidence of guilt. Jeff was the only man at odds with James Gosnell. However, after the $500 reward was announced, all eyes turned to Quincy Cramblett, and thereafter, every move Cramblett made was interpreted as a sign of guilt. Gregg pointed out the kindness and trust Gosnell seemed to exhibit toward Quincy, like dressing his sore hand, allowing him to bring the family home from Holmes Church and letting him sleep in his bed overnight. Dr. Hanna said Quincy's mother was sane. Her testimony that Quincy was home the night of the crime should be believed.

Gregg addressed the horse tracks. The tracks were not examined until two days later by the sheriff but should have been examined immediately. Many horses were at the Gosnell house after the murder and on Sunday, the following day. The men who measured the tracks guessed and used unreliable methods. The evidence that Quincy always shot crossfire was the strongest circumstance in the defendant's favor. The shooter did not stand in that position.

Gregg pointed out that Quincy went immediately to the Gosnell house when summoned after the murder. He continued, "Could the man who shot Gosnell have looked into the pallid face of his victim? No! Tell me Cramblett killed this man; it is as false as hell....I believe he is innocent. A guilty man generally flees....Flight is considered evidence of guilt.... Voluntary appearance is considered innocence."

Gregg ended with, "The state bypassed trying to prove Jeff Rainbow's whereabouts prior to the crime. The evidence against Quincy Cramblett was doubtful, shadowy and uncertain. Would this young man be offered up as a sacrifice, he asked." He warned the jury, "If there is only one man who doubted, he should stand as firm as the Rock of Gibraltar for justice."

At 3:20 p.m., prosecuting attorney Addison C. Lewis began his closing argument for the state. For over two and a half hours, he held the attention of everyone in the courtroom. He said it was unnecessary to warn the jury that the indictment was evidence of guilt. It was only a formal charge. On reasonable doubt, he cautioned the jury not to dare convict until satisfied beyond a reasonable doubt. Lewis said, "Neither I nor my associates are seeking a victim. We want no cheap laurels stained with blood. If, in a case like this, the guilty man is allowed to go free, we may as well kindle a fire, throw in your statutes and allow anarchy to reign."

Lewis believed taking up the points of evidence singly was not fair, and neither was asking the jury if they would convict on such testimony. He urged the jury to take up the points of evidence altogether.

Because Quincy was arrested for shooting a squirrel for his sick mother and the remarks Lewis himself made regarding Grafton's barn being burned, Lewis alerted the jury that they should not let these points prey upon their minds.

Lewis addressed Quincy's love affairs with Elva and Cora. Both girls professed their love to Quincy, but they also loved their father. Without any promises of marriage, Quincy's world grew dark to the point of desperation with the proposition that he and Cora commit suicide. Lewis added, "Had Cora told Cramblett she did not love him, James Gosnell might not have been murdered, but Cora might have been his victim."

Lewis, addressing other points of evidence, said the man who killed James Gosnell knew the premises and the family's habits. He maintained the dog didn't bark prior to the fatal shot because the dog knew Quincy Cramblett. If Rainbow had come, the dog would have barked with alarm. The shooter stood in a shadow and rested his gun on the fence just a few feet from Gosnell's back. The killer could not have shot crossfire because the light rays of the lamp would have struck him in the face.

Lewis continued to call attention to the absence of testimony by Quincy's brother Si Cramblett and his father, John Cramblett. "Where is Si Cramblett that he doesn't come forward and corroborate the statement of Quincy that the gun was taken over to Si's house four weeks before the murder?"

"Rise up, John Cramblett, and say a word on behalf of your son. No, John Cramblett is too dangerous a witness to put on the stand, because he would have to admit that he told Miller and Hall where the gun was and also who told him it was in the corn crib."

Lewis accused Quincy Cramblett of being deaf to the voice of Mt. Sinai, which said, "Thou shalt not kill." He pressed on powerfully, "Quincy Cramblett, you with this musket took James Gosnell's life."

Lewis asked the jury to "return a verdict of guilty, if convinced beyond a reasonable doubt that the defendant did the deed and said they owed it to the law, society and the family to find him guilty. If they wanted to be sympathetic, then dwell on the widow and orphaned daughters of James Gosnell, who have been ruthlessly robbed of a husband and father." Lewis thanked the jury for their patience and attention. He left the case in their hands. Court adjourned until 7:30 p.m. that evening.

When court reconvened after the dinner hour on April 7, 1900, the crowd was the largest seen during the trial. There was standing room only. As in previous sessions, women made up a greater percentage of the spectators, and many of them sat up front for a better view.

Judge Mansfield's charge to the jury took nearly forty minutes. He said, in part, "For the consequences of your verdict, faithfully rendered, you are not responsible. You will bear in mind that the accused is, by law, presumed to be innocent until his guilt shall be proved, and such presumption of innocence will continue until every element essential to constitute guilt shall be proved beyond a reasonable doubt.…The accused in a circumstantial case is entitled to the doubt. The accused cannot be lawfully convicted unless the evidence establishes his guilt beyond a reasonable doubt."

Mansfield continued, "You must look to all the evidence, and if that satisfies you of the defendant's guilt, you must say so. But if you are not fully satisfied but find only that there are strong probabilities of guilt, the only safe course is to acquit."

Mansfield defined for the jury the state statutes regarding murder in the first degree and if the deed was committed purposely and with premeditated malice. He explained in great detail the aspects of malice and added, "You will require that the testimony shall fully satisfy your minds, beyond a reasonable doubt, that the accused is the slayer of the person whose death, and the cause thereof, are the subjects of investigation before you."

Mansfield cautioned the jury, "Declarations of statements of the accused which have been admitted in evidence should be received by you with caution and should be carefully scrutinized, lest the language of the witness be substituted for that of the defendant, and for the further reason that they may have been imperfectly heard, defectively remembered or inaccurately related by the witness detailing the same."

The judge continued,

> *Circumstantial evidence is legal and competent in criminal cases; and if it is of such a character as to exclude every reasonable hypotheses other than that the defendant is guilty, it is entitled to the same weight as direct testimony; and where the State relies upon circumstantial evidence for a conviction, it is not enough that all the circumstances proved are consistent with and point to the defendant's guilt.*
>
> *Gentlemen, take the case. The responsibility is on you henceforth, and though it be a grave and serious one, yet I trust and believe that you will bring to the discharge of your duty, on the consideration of this case, careful and faithful effort to ascertain the truth to the end that you may a true verdict find according to the law and the evidence as it has been given to you in open court.*

At 8:10 p.m., the jury retired to consider the case. Most of the spectators waited patiently in the courtroom. When the jury bell rang at 10:10 p.m., the attorneys were summoned, and Cramblett was brought into court, where he sat down alone. No relatives were with him. They anxiously paced the corridors outside the courtroom, waiting on the verdict. Spectators whispered their predictions about the verdict. The jury members filed in at 10:20 p.m., and each answered when his name was called. A silence fell over the audience as they watched the prisoner and listened intently to hear the verdict.

"Gentlemen of the jury, have you agreed upon a verdict?" asked clerk Stokes.

"We have," replied the foreman, T.C. Wier of Toronto, who handed to the clerk the envelope containing the verdict.

Clerk Stokes opened the envelope and read slowly and impressively, "We, the jury, impaneled and sworn to well and truly try and true deliverance make between the State of Ohio and the prisoner at the bar, Quincy Cramblett, do find the defendant guilty of murder in the first degree, as he stands charged in the said indictment, and we, the jury, recommend mercy."

Hushed "ohs" were heard in all corners of the court room when the word *guilty* was uttered. Defense attorneys Gregg and Lewis asked for the jury to be polled. The clerk called each juror's name and asked, "Is this verdict your verdict?" Each man rose and replied, "It is." According to the amended law, "in a first-degree murder case when the jury recommended mercy, the penalty was life imprisonment in the penitentiary, without pardon, unless the prisoner was subsequently proven innocent beyond a reasonable doubt." Judge Mansfield thanked the jurors for their patience and said, "Gentlemen, you are discharged."

Quincy Cramblett maintained his calm, quiet behavior throughout the reading of the verdict. After the jury was dismissed, Quincy rose and started toward the jail entrance. The news of the verdict spread rapidly, and it soon became a topic of discussion with the Saturday night crowds on the streets of Steubenville. Public sympathy seemed to favor the prisoner. The verdict was criticized because there was not sufficient evidence, and it was thought that the verdict should not have been found on such evidence. The lawyers and others who had heard most of the evidence expected the verdict as rendered. All of the lawyers and court officers said there was more interest manifested in the Quincy Cramblett case than in any other murder trial in the history of Jefferson County.

7

PLANS, REFLECTIONS, COMMENTS

Although the law allowed three days to file for a new trial, defense attorneys Plummer P. Lewis and Henry Gregg filed immediately. Both attorneys believed so fervently in Quincy Cramblett's innocence that they were determined to continue the fight. They cited twenty-nine reasons to set aside the jury's guilty verdict against Quincy Cramblett. The verdict was against the law, against the evidence, against the weight of the evidence and not sustained by sufficient evidence.

Lewis and Gregg asserted that the court had erred in seventeen of the twenty-nine reasons as causes to set aside the guilty verdict. The court refused to allow a view of the premises where the murder occurred. Twenty-six exhibits, each labeled by a letter of the alphabet, were admitted in evidence over the objection of the defendant. Twenty-three of those exhibits were sent with the jury to be used in their deliberations over the objections of the defendant. Among the exhibits were the clothes of the murdered man and all the pieces and parts of the gun. Other errors related to procedural matters, such as: admission and rejection of evidence over objections, the judge's charge to the jury and the court's definition of reasonable doubt.

A strong feeling against the verdict evolved in Smithfield, Mt. Pleasant and other small towns in Jefferson County. The feeling was so strong in Mingo that there was talk of raising money to help pay the expenses of a new trial. The estimated cost of the first trial was $2,000. Other public opinion expressed was that since the jury recommended mercy, there must have been doubt in the jurors' minds as to Cramblett's guilt.

Reverend J.S. Reager, the pastor of the First Methodist Church, expressed his thoughts at length in his Sunday morning sermon. He attended most of the trial but missed the prosecutor's final statement. Reager had no criticism of the trial but said that "the verdict was not in harmony with the testimony."

Medical doctors who attended the trial during the week said that Quincy Cramblett's appearance suggested an "imbalanced mind," but the doctors never stated any reasons for their conclusion. Cramblett always appeared relaxed and never talked about the verdict, according to other prisoners.

On Wednesday, April 18, 1900, defense attorney Henry Gregg presented the motion for a new trial to the common pleas court. He said the horse tracks were not carefully inspected and that if the horse was Quincy's, it was never shown who rode it. He believed strongly that John Cramblett and Jeff Rainbow should have been called to the witness stand. The state skillfully avoided this action because if Jeff had gone on the witness stand, "it would have opened a door which was dangerous."

Defense attorney Plummer Lewis learned that the verdict was a surprise to those who attended the trial, and they were as competent to judge as the jury. Lewis hesitated to criticize the jury but felt the court would not allow this verdict to stand on such evidence in a civil case for damages, let alone on a first-degree murder charge, where evidence must show guilt beyond a reasonable doubt. He said the mere fact that the jury recommended mercy showed that they had doubt. Both Gregg and Lewis were intent on proving Cramblett's innocence.

Prosecuting attorney A.C. Lewis emphasized the strength of the evidence that was presented in his argument to the jury. He believed that the verdict in the case was simply the outcome of the evidence. At the beginning of the trial, the jury was prejudiced in favor of the prisoner. Lewis added that it was an insult to the jury members' intelligence to think they had been swayed by the arguments of the attorneys.

John Cook, for the state, said that from the evidence alone, no other conclusion could be arrived at except the guilt of Quincy Cramblett. He pointed out the falsehoods made by Cramblett as important points in the case. Cook believed the evidence in this case was much stronger than the evidence in cases where convictions were secured.

Judge Mansfield remanded Quincy Cramblett to jail and announced that he would consider the arguments of the attorneys regarding a new trial. In less than two weeks, Mansfield ruled for a new trial but confirmed that it would be several months away. The local public gave themselves credit for helping obtain the decision. In the meantime, Quincy remained in the sweltering Jefferson County Jail all summer.

Further investigation and preparation for the second trial continued during the summer months. One report told of a man who passed through Martins Ferry before daylight the morning after the murder and gave details about the murder that no one would have known. According to witnesses, the man practically said he shot Gosnell. The story was not believed, so the man disappeared into West Virginia. The winds of change blew constantly during the interim and up to the opening day of the second trial.

PART III

THE SECOND TRIAL

8

JURY SELECTION, PROSECUTION

In September 1900, attorneys Henry Gregg and Plummer P. Lewis sent a request to Judge Mansfield to permit them to retire from the Quincy Cramblett murder case. The men had learned that the Cramblett family had hired attorney Dio Rogers to defend Quincy in the second trial. Rogers was joined by Emmett E. Erskine, who had represented Cramblett at the initial hearing in Mt. Pleasant in November 1899. Prosecuting attorney Addison C. Lewis and attorney John M. Cook remained in place for the state.

Near the end of September, clerk Stokes issued subpoenas for 116 defense witnesses. The state summoned 60 witnesses. Stokes, in conjunction with the sheriff, drew names from the jury wheel and delivered the summons.

Court opened on Monday, October 22, 1900, but no judge was present. Everyone waited for about two hours before anything transpired. Rumors were whispered in the corridors that Judge Mansfield would not try the case again. By 11:00 a.m., Judge Jesse W. Hollingsworth of St. Clairsville, Belmont County, had arrived, and to the surprise of everyone, he announced that he would try the case. Judge Mansfield had family estate business to settle, and he had recently written to Hollingsworth to ask him to act as judge. Jesse Hollingsworth, a large man with white hair and mustache, served as the common pleas judge and was well liked and respected in Eastern Ohio. The state and defense accepted him as the judge to try the case. At that point, it was time for a noon meal.

Court reconvened after lunch. The sheriff brought Quincy into the courtroom. Seated beside Quincy were his parents, John and Mary Cramblett, and his sister and brother-in-law, Mary Josephine and Addison McClain.

The Gosnell women were not present. The jury selection process began and lasted all afternoon and all day Tuesday, October 23, plus Wednesday, October 24. When court adjourned on Wednesday, the special venire of sixty names was exhausted, and still, not enough men had been chosen for a jury. That evening, another special venire of sixty names was drawn from the wheel. The sheriff and his deputy started at 4:00 a.m. on Thursday, October 25, to summon the sixty men whose names were drawn Wednesday night.

Court opened at 9:00 a.m. on Thursday, October 25, but none of the men summoned arrived until after 10:00 a.m. The jury selection process continued all day. When court adjourned Thursday evening, there were still only ten jurors selected—twelve were needed. A third venire of twenty names was drawn, and the men were summoned on Friday, October 26. Out of that group, the final two jurors were selected, and a jury was seated by noon.

JUDGE JESSE W. HOLLINGSWORTH.

Judge Jesse W. Hollingsworth of St. Clairsville, Belmont County, Ohio, presided over the second first-degree murder trial in the Quincy Cramblett case. *From the* Steubenville Herald Star, *"Charge of the Court," November 12, 1900.*

The twelve-member jury consisted of George Lawson, a farmer from Salem Township; William C. Yeagley, a merchant from New Somerset; Joseph Peoples an engineer from Port Homer; James Lawrence, a hotel keeper from Hammondsville; S.Z. Alexander, a farmer from Knox Township; Ross D. Stark, a farmer from Wintersville; Ross P. Frederick and Thomas S. Saunders, both farmers from Island Creek Township; Joseph Bowers and David E. Andrews, both farmers from Cross Creek Township; and Oliver J. Brown and Joseph McCullough, both farmers from Fernwood. After consulting with prosecuting attorney Addison Lewis, Judge Hollingsworth announced that he would adjourn court until 2:45 p.m. to allow the attorneys time to prepare their statements for the jury.

The court reconvened at 2:45 p.m., with the courtroom so crowded that many spectators had to stand. Not unlike the first trial, a multitude of women attended to hear more of the love drama surrounding Cora and Quincy and to see the handsome prisoner.

Quincy's brother Si Cramblett, with other relatives, sat beside Quincy. Widow Mary Gosnell, attired in black, along with her daughters Cora and

Elva, sat behind the state's attorneys. The jury was sworn in, and prosecuting attorney Addison Lewis proceeded with his opening statement.

Lewis read the indictment, which charged Quincy Cramblett with the premeditated murder of James H. Gosnell on the night of November 4, 1899. Gosnell was at home with his family and sitting with his back to a kitchen window when he was shot. Six bullets entered his body and killed him instantly. The Gosnell women sobbed quietly upon hearing the tragic details again. Lewis continued and said Quincy had courted both Elva and Cora Gosnell and proposed marriage to each lady but was turned down by both young women. Lewis continued with his statements to the jury until closing time, which was late in the day. Court adjourned.

Court reopened Saturday, October 27, with few spectators present. The afternoon session was packed, around 90 percent of the crowd being women. Quincy, as usual, sat motionless without any telling facial expression or body language. When Cora Gosnell was called to the witness stand in the afternoon, she was questioned about the events of the night of her father's murder. Cora repeated her previous statements from the first trial without alteration. She didn't notice other people examining the window where the shot was fired or asking questions about the murder. She felt that Quincy did not react any differently from the other people by not inquiring about the murder.

Cora said she had met Quincy at Holmes Church when gatherings of the Epworth League were held for young people. Quincy's numerous proposals of marriage always drew the same refusal from her. She did not promise to marry him at that time or sometime in the future. Her sister Clara's marriage to Will Gutshall prompted a firestorm with her father, and Cora felt that one such upheaval in the family was enough. Cora never witnessed any unkind words pass between her father and Quincy. She always heard her father invite Quincy back to visit.

Quincy promised to do the best for her during his proposals, but she continued to refuse him. He suggested that they commit suicide together, but she was not ready to die that way. One week before the murder, Quincy suggested that they keep company for the night at Micajah Moore's house. He assured her the old folks would not find out. But Cora knew her family would find out and that there would be trouble. Despite all of the negative answers she gave to Quincy's requests, Cora answered emphatically that she loved Quincy and knew that he loved her.

Cora confirmed that when Quincy came to the house after the murder, he went with her to view her father's body. At one point, he even helped ice down Mr. Gosnell's body, as was customary at the time.

On cross-examination, defense attorney Erskine prodded Cora to recall Quincy's words from his first marriage proposal. She couldn't remember. Erskine persisted and then asked if she had gotten off her horse the last morning she saw Quincy at the cow gap. "No," she said. Lewis forged on and asked if she kissed Quincy. She denied kissing Quincy that morning and said she only leaned down from the saddle when Quincy kissed her.

David Gotshall, a neighbor and the next witness called to the stand, lived about seven hundred yards from the Gosnells. After the shooting, he said he heard screams coming from the Gosnell house. He rode to the house and found Jeff Rainbow present. Gotshall stayed the remainder of the evening and noticed that after Quincy arrived, he did not ask any questions about the murder or examine the window, as others had done. David Gotshall testified that most of the men at the Gosnell house after the murder were afraid to go outside unless two or three went together. But he said Quincy was not afraid and went out alone to bring in coal or water. However, Gotshall confessed to being a little deaf. David Gotshall's wife testified to the same statements given by her husband, David.

Judge Hollingsworth took time to lecture the attorneys. He observed that the attorneys seemed to want the last word with the witnesses and said if those tactics continued, it would take an endless amount of time to try the case. He cautioned them to conduct the examination according to the rules. It was now late Saturday afternoon. Judge Hollingsworth adjourned court until 9:00 a.m. on Monday, October 29, 1900.

The court proceedings grew more complicated each day. While a great percentage of the testimony was repeated from the first trial, new twists of fact or fiction came forth during the second trial. When court reconvened on Monday morning, more witnesses testified. *Steubenville Herald Star* photographer J.H. Andrews was called to the stand. He identified photographs he took of the Gosnell premises. An objection to the photographs being introduced as evidence was sustained.

Ella Grimm, another neighbor, testified that she saw Quincy at the Gosnell home on Sunday, the day after the murder. She commented to him, "Someone must have had a terrible grudge against James Gosnell to kill him." Quincy replied, "It takes all kinds of people to make a world." Grimm saw nothing else that aroused her suspicion of Quincy.

The former coroner J.A. Fisher described the scene of the murder when he arrived at the Gosnell home on the morning of Sunday, November 5, 1899. Charles Gosnell, the son of the murdered man, and Dr. Barkhurst turned over the bullets taken from the victim's body, plus one bullet found by Deputy Sheriff George Moore. Fisher said he had found footprints near the paling fence located a few feet from the window through which the fatal shot was fired.

The great horseshoe controversy occupied a lot of time in the second trial. Descriptions of the horse tracks were confusing, contradictory and involved considerable guesswork. During testimony, three versions of the horse's tracks were described: the horse suspected of being the murderer's had three shoes on and one missing off of the left front foot; the horse had four feet shod; and the horse had three feet without a shoe and one foot with a shoe. Measurements of the horse tracks were taken by various unreliable methods, such as using a stick and a lead pencil. The measuring implements were destroyed after the first trial.

On a bank across Perrin Run and about three hundred feet above the Gosnell house, former coroner J.A. Fisher found horse tracks where the suspected shooter's horse had been tied. He measured the tracks with a lead pencil. Later, he measured Quincy's horse's tracks, and they corresponded exactly. Upon closer examination of Quincy's horse, Fisher found its left front hoof was unshod, but the other three feet had shoes.

Sheriff Porter testified that he examined the horse tracks in detail on Sunday, the day after the murder, and even got down on his hands and knees to inspect the tracks more closely. He followed the tracks along Perrin Run, where the horse crossed the run to where it had been hitched. The horse had no shoe on its left front foot and matched the tracks of Quincy's horse. He concurred with all of Fisher's testimony. Porter was asked if the guilty verdict of the first trial had influenced his testimony, as his costs were determined by a guilty verdict. The sheriff assured the court that the collection of his fees did not influence his testimony.

On Sunday, November 5, 1899, the day after the murder, William Wilkinson said he examined the horse tracks near Perrin Run to the corner where the horse was hitched. He said the tracks showed there were four shoes on the horse. He said that if he claimed in the first trial that he had followed the tracks only forty or fifty feet, he was mistaken and did not understand the question. Warren King, who was with Wilkinson, said they followed the tracks for fifty to seventy-five feet and that they pointed to a horse with four shoes. When asked about what he testified to at the first trial, he said could not remember.

Charles King examined the horse tracks the same day. He said he only saw tracks from the horse's front feet. One foot was shod, and the other was not.

Constable Stant McMasters, under oath, said that he obtained horse track measurements from Coroner Fisher and gave the information to William Cheffy the day after the murder. Cheffy testified that he was given a stick that had been used to measure the alleged shooter's horse tracks. He examined the horse tracks at Jeff Rainbow's barn and, after measuring, found them to match exactly. During further questioning, Cheffy became extremely confused about which front foot of Quincy's horse had a shoe on it and what he had testified to at the first trial.

Walter Meek testified that he saw the horse tracks on Sunday but did not examine said tracks until Monday along with William Cheffy and Stant McMasters. They measured the tracks and went to a field where they measured Jeff Rainbow's horse's tracks. It was a match. The men also measured Jeff's horse's tracks at his barn gate. Everything matched. The horse had three shoes off and one shoe on.

Several witnesses could not remember what they said about the horse tracks in their testimony at the first trial. No witness actually saw a horse tied in the alleged specific location near Perrin Run the night of November 4, 1899, when James Gosnell was murdered.

Clayton Carter, a neighborhood farmer and second cousin to Mrs. Gosnell and Quincy, testified that three weeks after the murder, he and George Gosnell, the nephew of the murdered man, measured horse tracks under manure where a horse was supposed to have been hitched the night of the murder. The stick with which they had measured the tracks had been thrown away by Carter's wife after the first trial. A heavy rain fell during this time, which prevented further measurement. In the meantime, Carter had a horse newly shod before attorney Erskine examined the tracks. The tracks were determined to be those of Carter's newly shod horse. Erskine was sworn in and concurred with Carter's testimony.

Neighborhood residents Thomas Marchbank and Hugh Best testified that they believed the horse in question had its left front hoof unshod and other three feet with shoes. Best also said that the shot he heard on November 4 was not from a rifle but could have been from a horse pistol. Marchbank's wife, Hyantha, was also a second cousin to both Mrs. Gosnell and Quincy Cramblett.

Charles Irwin, a marshal of Martins Ferry, Belmont County, and R.A. Lindermann, a former marshal of Martins Ferry, examined the horse tracks on the Monday after the murder. Irwin could not tell whether the horse was shod or not. Lindermann saw only two front hoof tracks, and only one had a shoe. Among the tracks Clayton Hoge examined, he saw one track that was distinctly void of a shoe.

Witness George Gosnell, the nephew of the murdered man, said he stayed at the Gosnell home several months after the crime. Mrs. Gosnell and her daughters went to live with her son, Charles. George revealed in the first trial and restated that a few days after the murder, two men from Martins Ferry had come to the house and asked to speak with Quincy. George obliged and took the horse and buggy to bring Quincy to the Gosnell house. On their way back, Quincy inquired of George if people suspected him of the murder. George assured Quincy that officers might suspect anybody. Quincy told George that if the family stuck by him, he would be alright, but if they didn't, his cake would be dough. Upon further questioning, George said he had known Quincy for over ten years, and they had spent a good deal of time together in the past two years. George was asked about a penholder he found outside the kitchen window where the fatal shot was fired. It looked like one he had seen at his uncle's house but couldn't say for sure if it was the same one shown in the exhibit.

James McMannis, a justice of peace and former postmaster, repeated what he said in the first trial. He found a black substance, which he thought was felt, lodged in the wallpaper across the room from where Gosnell had been shot. Particles of window glass were lodged in the black substance. McMannis repeated the conversation he had with Quincy at Robert Chamber's drugstore in Mt. Pleasant, during which Quincy revealed that he cut wads with a knife out of an old black felt hat.

George Moore, the court bailiff, helped search the Cramblett house after the murder. He found a rifle along with a bullet in a bullet pouch. When cross-examined, he confessed that he did not try to fit the bullet into the gun, but he said he thought maybe it might go in the barrel. He guessed that the bullet might fit in the gun—similar to measuring the horse tracks with a pencil or stick.

The last two witnesses on Monday made a variety of statements about the alleged gun and its bullets. With his account book, Robert Nichols proved that he worked at the Gosnell farm on October 21, two weeks prior to the murder. He said he saw the musket at the Gosnell house and that it was the same one shown in the exhibit. George Thompson testified that he worked with Nichols on October 21 at the Gosnell farm. He put an iron ramrod down the barrel of the gun in question and found it had a two-inch load inside. When young Nichols was cross-examined, he was so nervous that he could hardly speak. He was questioned about his testimony at the preliminary hearing, and he could not remember anything about it. Nor could he move his body at the moment. He continued to be in a trance and sat in the witness box until court was adjourned for the day and the courtroom was cleared.

On Tuesday, October 30, 1900, the parade of witnesses continued. Deputy Sheriff D.S. McMasters, the constable of Mt. Pleasant Township at the time of the murder, said he spoke with Quincy a few days after the murder. McMasters asked Quincy if he knew his horse's tracks matched the tracks found near the murder scene and that people suspected him as the shooter. Quincy replied that his horse might have been there, but he was not. He said he "had no lovey, no sweetheart" at the Gosnells', never kept company with the Gosnell girls and that they were just neighbors. McMasters asked Quincy the whereabouts of the missing musket. Quincy said it had been at his brother Si's house for about a month.

Deputy McMasters said that when he examined Quincy's shoulders, he thought one of them looked swollen. He then asked Quincy to go with him to Mt. Pleasant to be examined by Dr. McGlenn. Quincy cooperated and removed his shirt so the doctor could examine his shoulder for possible bruises or injury caused by kickback from a firing gun. Dr. McGlenn found no such evidence.

Noah Arnold, a witness from Belmont County, testified that he shot the same musket when coon hunting about a year prior. He was left with a bloodied nose and a black and blue shoulder that lasted several days. William Drake was present when McMasters questioned Quincy and confirmed all the deputy's testimony. Drake added that Quincy said he always shot crossfire because he could not shut one of his eyes. If shooting crossfire, the shooter would place the firearm against his left shoulder and use the right eye to take aim.

Seventy-five-year-old Lavina Rainbow, Jeff's mother, said she heard a shot between 7:00 p.m. and 8:00 p.m. on the night of the murder. She went outside, heard screams and then heard a horse coming up the road from the Gosnells'. She could not see the rider because of the darkness, and the horse was traveling very fast. She went back into the house. Jeff eventually returned and told her of the shooting. When cross-examining, the defense asked Mrs. Rainbow what time Jeff returned, and the state immediately objected. In a lengthy review, Judge Hollingsworth instructed the defense attorneys that the rule of law regarding cross-examination was that witnesses could be questioned only on subjects that they had been asked about in direct examination. Lavina Rainbow was excused.

Witness James Noble, a farmer from Smithfield Township, said he talked with Quincy on Tuesday, November 7, 1899, the day of James Gosnell's funeral. Quincy asked Noble why people suspected him of the murder. Noble assured Quincy that his stories didn't match, and it was catching up with him. Quincy uttered a string of excuses, saying that he never thought of going with the Gosnell girls. A few days before the murder, Quincy's horse was ridden to the Gosnells' by Davie Rennard and, at that time, lost its left front shoe. Plus, the musket was at his brother's house for over a month. Noble quoted Quincy's last remark: "I am innocent, and the day of judgment will show it." Defense attorney Erskine repeated the quote with emphasis. That prompted an immediate objection from the state. Judge Hollingsworth warned that side remarks were highly improper at this time.

As cross-examination continued, the effort to confuse Noble about his comments made him angry. When asked if he was going about trying to find out what the defense witnesses knew, he defiantly said, "No, sir, you have been on my heels."

Referring to the Pinkerton Detective Agency, Erskine asked, "Don't they call you Pinkerton Jim?"

Noble shot back quickly, "You started it."

The crowd broke out in uproarious laughter. After order was restored, Judge Hollingsworth warned the crowd they must keep quiet if they wanted to stay. He promised to clear the courtroom if order was not preserved, and he instructed the bailiff to bring to the bar anyone who violated the order.

Witness William Thompson lived about three miles from the Cramblett family and said that on the day Quincy talked to Noble, he saw Quincy riding to his brother Si's house. When Quincy rode home, he and Thompson had a brief conversation, but Thompson did not see anything suspicious in Quincy's behavior.

Court adjourned for lunch.

When court reconvened on Tuesday afternoon, October 30, witness Dr. S. Osborne Barkhurst testified. He was a second cousin to both Mrs. Gosnell and Quincy Cramblett. The doctor displayed and explained a drawing of the wounds he found on James Gosnell's body. He said he knew Quincy all his life. Barkhurst described an old army musket that he owned and used for hunting. Once when he was hunting, he accidentally shot out one of his eyes and, simultaneously, a two-inch hole was shot in the hat he was wearing. The musket scattered shot more than a shotgun and kicked when it was heavily loaded. Some modifications had been made to parts of the musket. He divested himself of the musket, and it fell into the hands of the Cramblett family. Barkhurst recognized the hammer of the musket because of a special mark it had, but he was not certain of the other parts on exhibit, as it had been seven or eight years since he had seen the musket. The defense objected to the exhibition of broken gun parts to the jury. They were overruled.

Controversy and questions regarding the whereabouts of the musket after the murder of James Gosnell continued to be a focus in witness testimonies. New evidence came forth. The prosecution pressed forward with William Miller, Quincy's brother-in-law, who testified that he was present at John Cramblett's house the week after the murder. A family meeting occurred with the parents, John and Mary Cramblett; their son Si and his wife, Emma; their daughter, Josie McLain; and Quincy. When the group proceeded to the barn to get a horse, Quincy asked why people suspected him of the murder and said, "No one saw me down there, and they will have to prove I was there." John Cramblett warned Quincy, "Don't speak so loud; somebody up in the barn might hear you."

A few days after the meeting, Miller was at his father-in-law's house when he said he was directed by John Cramblett to look for a musket in the corn crib. That statement was ordered to be stricken from the record.

Miller testified that he entered the highly piled corn in the corn crib and, after a brief search, found the musket. He passed the musket out of the corn crib to Milton Hall. Hall found a sledgehammer, took the musket under the barn and smashed it to pieces. Miller bent the gun barrel in half. He said Hall went to the house to get a feed sack and comforter. All of the gun parts were put in the feed sack and wrapped with the comforter. With the comforter, sack and contents, Miller started for home three miles away on Piney Fork Creek. Once he reached home, he proceeded to burn the wood pieces in his cookstove. He took the metal pieces to Jim Elliott's woods, less than a mile away, and buried them under various logs. Before Christmas 1899, Miller and Hall revisited the site to retrieve the pieces and parts of the gun. They tied the collection around Hall's body under his coat, and Hall took it home. At his farm home near York, Hall proceeded to put the bent musket barrel down a well.

Milt Hall's testimony corroborated Miller's regarding the discovery of the gun in the corn crib, its destruction, the hiding of its parts in the woods, the retrieval of the parts and the placement of the gun barrel down the well at his home. At a later date, Hall witnessed Deputy Sheriff Ross Stone take the gun barrel from the well. After a short recess, the state offered the gun barrel and other gun parts as evidence. The defense objected but was overruled.

David Renner was recalled and testified that he was at the Gosnell home on Wednesday before the murder and that he had hitched his horse in the stable. No inquiry was made about the description of his horse or why he was at the Gosnells'.

Several men testified that they had always seen Quincy Cramblett shoot crossfire, resting the gun against his left shoulder and using his right eye to aim with his right foot forward. Those witnesses were Harry Paxton, Leander Fulton, George Fulton, Elias Fulton, Nathan O. Phipps, William Fisher, Sherman Fulton, Errett Dallas and Wallace DeOrman.

After a half-hour wait for a witness who did not appear, the prosecution decided not to call said witness and rested its case at noon on Wednesday, October 31, 1900. The spectators were few in number.

9

DEFENSE

The defense swore in 209 witnesses. If the defense called all the witnesses, the reporters did not include their names in the newspaper articles. At the request of the state's attorneys, witnesses remained out of the courtroom until called to the witness stand. Character witnesses for the accused were called to testify on the afternoon of Wednesday, October 31. The same questions were asked of each witness. How long did the witness know Quincy Cramblett? Was the accused kindhearted and humane? Did the accused have a reputation for peace and quietness? Most of the replies to the questions were positive and supportive of Quincy Cramblett. A few answers were more in-depth about Cramblett's personality and his religious life.

William Judkins, the superintendent of the Methodist Episcopal Sunday school in Smithfield for thirty-five years, said he had known Quincy for thirty years and that Quincy frequently attended Sunday school when he lived near Smithfield. John Cheffy added that Quincy had been the Sunday school treasurer. Miss Latie Reid of Mt. Pleasant said Quincy was converted four or five years prior during a series of religious meetings held at the Dillonvale Presbyterian Chapel. Oliver Bracken concurred about Quincy's conversion and thought the young man was different after that event. Bascom M. Hastings said he belonged to the Holmes Methodist Church, where Quincy attended. The defense attorney asked Hastings if the Methodists in the country didn't get pretty well acquainted. Judge Hollingsworth immediately ruled out the question and admonished the attorneys to keep church and state separate.

The following witnesses testified that they knew Quincy Cramblett and said that he had a good reputation: William Hammond, Joseph Kithcart, Clara Mitchell, John Galbraith, Robert Chambers, A.U. Moore, Susan (Glover) Comly, Lizzie Comly, Eva Bracken, Reverend S.A. Peregoy, Samuel Vail, Charles Ingler, John L. Barkhurst Sr., John Cheffey, Reverend Salmon, William Carter, James Mulholland, Elizabeth Neil, Oliver Bracken, William Rennard, John F. Cheffy, Plummer Haines, William B. Shane and U.M. Case.

Ellsworth Barkhurst, Quincy's second cousin, testified about a conversation he had with John Cramblett, Quincy's father. John allegedly told Ellsworth Barkhurst that Quincy was short-tempered and not a very good boy. The prosecutor asked what Mr. Cramblett said about Quincy's treatment of horses. Barkhurst replied that John Cramblett said Quincy was rough on horses. The prosecutor urged the witness to say what else Mr. Cramblett had told him. The defense strongly objected, and it was sustained. Similar to Ellsworth Barkhurst, Lewis Castner was cross-examined about Quincy's character. He said John Cramblett had told him that Quincy wasn't using him right. The defense objected, and the remark was stricken from the record.

The ever-present great horseshoe controversy and the question about whether Quincy Cramblett shot crossfire were target queries for men called to the witness stand. The questioning consumed a considerable amount of time in the courtroom on Thursday and Friday, November 1 and 2. Some men who testified at the first trial now either forgot what they had previously said or were totally confused about what they said.

William Cheffy, like other witnesses before him, was confused about the horse tracks. He said the horse tracks he saw had a shoe on the right front foot and no shoes on the other feet. After Cheffy acquired the stick the coroner had used to measure the horse tracks, he went to Jeff Rainbow's place to measure the feet on Jeff's horse. They were exactly the same size, according to him. When he was cross-examined, he confessed that he was confused at the first trial when he said the left front foot was shod. Cheffy said he met Cramblett on the road to the Gosnell home the morning after the murder. At that time, he noticed that Cramblett's horse had a shoe off its left front foot and a piece broken out of another hoof. But now he said he knew it was the right front foot that was shod. He recognized the mistake when he left the courtroom after the first trial. Cheffy stated that Dr. Barkhurst was his brother-in-law. Cheffy's wife, Martha, was the doctor's sister. Sibling, cousin and other relationships were revealed throughout both trials.

Charles Irwin, the marshal at Martins Ferry, testified that he was at the Gosnell home the Monday after the murder. After a careful examination of the tracks, he could not tell if the horse was shod or not. R.A. Lindermann, a former marshal in Martins Ferry, was with Irwin when the tracks were examined. He said he saw only two tracks of front hoofs and that one was shod. Clayton Hoge of Mt. Pleasant testified with confusing statements. He saw horse tracks in several locations but did not examine the ground where the horse was allegedly hitched to the fence.

The time arrived for testimony by Quincy Cramblett's family members. Quincy's brother, Josiah, known as Si, was the first to take the stand. Si stated that at the time of the Gosnell murder, he lived about four miles south of Bloomfield, known as Bloomingdale today. He had a public sale on Thursday, November 2, which was two days before the murder. Quincy came to help him with the sale. Si testified that sometime before the sale, he brought the musket home from his father's house. He left it in various places, like in a wagon, in the granary and in the haymow. His wife, Emma, did not like guns around because once she had a gun go off accidentally near her feet. Emma did not know that Si had a gun with a load stuck in it in their attic. Si said he brought the musket home to scare thieves who were stealing his chickens. When shown the parts of the gun that were found in the well and the woods, Si could not say for sure if he had ever seen the parts before or if they were from the old musket. Some parts, he thought, bore a resemblance to those from the old musket.

The prosecutor asked, "How did you expect to scare chicken thieves with that empty musket hidden down in the barn?"

On cross-examination, Si testified that Quincy called at his house a few days after the murder. They talked about the sale, and then Quincy revealed that he was suspected of committing the murder. Si advised Quincy not to speak about it again. The next day, Si and Emma went to visit Mr. and Mrs. Cramblett. Although no meeting was planned, it just so happened that Quincy, Josie McClain and William Miller were there.

Si Cramblett's testimony continued. While at the family gathering, Si asked his brother-in-law, William Miller, if he saw a gun in Si's attic on the day of the sale. Miller said he did see a gun when he put his gun upstairs in the unused room. Si then told Miller, "If you are to testify, tell about putting your old gun beside my shotgun upstairs." When asked if he remembered Will Drake and James Walker calling at his home the Thursday after the murder, Si claimed he did not remember. In the meantime, Drake told Si they were there, but Si said he couldn't remember.

The prosecutor inquired about James Noble's visit to Si's house. Si told Noble that the missing musket was in the haymow. Noble asked to see it, but Si refused and asked Noble if he had a search warrant or legal documents giving him the right to ask questions. The next day, Si discovered that the locks on several of his buildings had been broken. To his surprise, the musket was missing.

Prosecutor Lewis continued to probe, "Did you have that musket up there at your house more than two weeks before James Gosnell was killed?

"Yes, sir."

"You are positive of that?"

"I told you I had it up there about three weeks before."

Si testified that no one saw him get the musket out of his buggy the day he brought it from his father's house.

When court opened on Friday morning, November 2, 1900, Judge Hollingsworth announced that because of the strange circumstances surrounding this case, he would admit into evidence statements made by James Gosnell, the deceased, relating his feelings toward the prisoner, Quincy Cramblett. Witness Noah Arnold was recalled and testified that Gosnell told him Quincy "was as nice and accommodating young man as he ever had anything to do with."

At long last, John Cramblett, Quincy's father, took the witness stand. In response to questions, he testified that Quincy was thirty-three years old. He acknowledged that the musket had been at Si's house for two or more weeks before the murder. Mr. Cramblett bought cattle at Si's sale, and he and Quincy drove them to his farm after the sale. Mr. Cramblett then rode to Adena to get their mail. His wife prepared dinner, and the three ate together. They read the mail and newspaper, after which Quincy removed his boots and clothing, closed the stairway door and proceeded up the stairs to bed.

The witness and his wife prepared for bed. They slept in the sitting room, which was the only way to access the upstairs area where Quincy slept. He did not see Quincy again until after Jeff Rainbow knocked at the door around midnight, told him of Gosnell's death and said Quincy was wanted at the Gosnell house. The witness said he called up the stairs twice before Quincy appeared; he said Quincy came downstairs and dressed quickly. Quincy could not believe the news. The witness said he and Quincy rode to Charles Gosnell's home and found no one there, after which Quincy proceeded to James Gosnell's house.

In answer to further questions, John Cramblett testified that the musket had been in the family for about twenty years. Quincy had the right to use it whenever he wished. The witness said he did not use the musket because it had a load stuck in it. After being shown the piece of tin that had been burned off the musket, he said it was wider than the piece that had been tacked around the gunstock. The thumb piece on the hammer was higher than the one on his old musket. He could not identify the gun barrel as the one on his old musket. He did not know if the gun was loaded or not when Nichols and Thompson worked at his place in October. He denied telling Miller and Hall on November 27, 1899, to go get the gun and destroy it. But he said Miller and Hall came to him in the field that day and told him they found the gun, to which he replied, "Go away and let me alone, gun and all."

John Cramblett was asked if he knew John Frazier. He responded that he knew several John Fraziers and that two of them were neighbors. He denied talking to John Frazier on the night of the murder. Finally, the John Frazier who was being referred to was brought into the courtroom, identified as exhibit Z, and John Cramblett again did not remember seeing him on the night of the murder.

Early expectations were that the cross-examinations would be completed by this day, Friday, November 2, 1900, unless the court admitted evidence of Jeff Rainbow's threats made against James Gosnell. While few spectators were present in the morning, attendance increased for the afternoon session. Spectators remembered that it had been one year since the murder of James H. Gosnell had occurred on November 4, 1899.

After a lunch break, John Cramblett returned to the witness stand. He could not remember testifying before the grand jury. His testimony before the grand jury was read to him by the stenographer, and he said he may have so testified. Regarding the initial hearing held in Mt. Pleasant, Cramblett said he did not go because he did not receive a subpoena. Immediately, he said he did get a subpoena but was told not to go.

John Cramblett denied that he had conversation with Miller and Hall at any time about the gun; that he told Miller and Hall to look for the musket in the corn crib and that if they found it to destroy it; and that Miller told him about how he destroyed the gun. All through the cross-examination, the defense objected to every question, but each time, it was overruled.

James H. Gosnell and Jeff Rainbow had an ongoing dispute about the fence line between their farms. At the Saturday court session, the state recalled Micajah Moore and asked if he could identify a letter he saw Jeff Rainbow reading as the same letter he saw on the township clerk's desk. Moore said he could not identify it. The state then asked if the bill was written on November 29, 1899, twenty-five days after the murder. In a surprise move, the prosecutor pulled the bill from his pocket and showed it to Moore. The letter head had been torn off, but the date was still shown. The witness said the writing looked like that of the township clerk.

Court stenographer Campbell was recalled to the stand and asked by the defense what Jeff Rainbow testified to at the preliminary hearing. The state objected and had Jeff Rainbow brought into court to show that he was present and could testify for himself. The large crowd of spectators twisted and stretched their necks to see just what the much-talked-about Jeff Rainbow looked like. Much to their disappointment, they stared at this little, short man who seemed to be terribly embarrassed by all of the attention he was getting. If Rainbow testified, the press did not cover it.

The afternoon of Monday, November 5, 1900, was devoted exclusively to asking questions about what Jeff Rainbow said in a multitude of situations.

Charles Gosnell, the murdered man's son, was recalled to the witness stand. In reply to the state's questions, he said the township trustees employed him to build the Rainbow part of the fence and paid him seventy-five dollars. He completed the fence in October 1899, before his father's death. While he was building the fence, he said Jeff Rainbow came to the site a couple of times. The defense asked what Rainbow said. The state objected. The attorneys engaged in a bickering session over the admission of testimony, which would show that Jeff Rainbow had made threats against James Gosnell, for whose murder Quincy Cramblett was being tried. Defense attorney Erskine said, "We will make a stronger case of circumstantial evidence against Rainbow than the state makes against Cramblett." The state was determined to keep Rainbow from testifying.

Judge Hollingsworth intervened and announced that since it was 4:00 p.m., he would adjourn court until Monday morning to allow the witnesses to go home that Sunday.

On Monday, November 5, 1900, court opened with few spectators, but as usual, attendance increased for the afternoon session. The national election fell in the middle of the second trial on Tuesday, November 6. Judge Hollingsworth announced that he would adjourn court at 4:00 p.m. on Monday so witnesses could have the opportunity to go home and vote.

Republican incumbent William McKinley and Democrat William Jennings Bryan were the presidential candidates. Court would reconvene at 1:30 p.m. on Tuesday, November 6. If witnesses were residents of the southernmost part of Jefferson County, the distance to the court was up to twenty-five or more miles over poor roads. Some, if not all, of the witnesses took the train. The court could not take chances on allowing the twelve jury members to leave, so they had to lose their vote in this election. The jury was composed of ten Republicans and two Democrats.

The many witnesses who took the stand on Monday were all asked questions about encounters they had with Jeff Rainbow and what Rainbow said. Besides the construction of the property line fence, other questions were posed about a horse pistol owned by Jeff Rainbow and Quincy's personality. When asked what Jeff Rainbow said to each witness during an encounter, objection was rapidly called, followed by a sustention from the judge. Charles Gosnell was recalled to the stand and asked what Jeff Rainbow said to him when he was building the fence. Objection. Sustained.

Charles Irwin, a marshal of Martins Ferry, and R.A. Lindermuth, a former marshal of Martins Ferry, were called separately to the witness stand. The two men had a talk with Jeff Rainbow on Monday after the murder. The men were asked what Rainbow said. Objection. Sustained. James McBride was recalled to the witness stand. He was asked again what Jeff Rainbow said to him twenty years ago regarding what he would do to anyone who touched a rail on the fence between his farm and the Fleming farm. Objection. Sustained.

A horse pistol allegedly owned by Jeff Rainbow emerged as an item of surprise evidence in the second trial. J.O. Henry testified that he had known Jeff Rainbow his entire life. Henry was asked what he knew about Jeff owning a horse pistol. Objection. Sustained.

Elsie Crossley, a neighbor of the Rainbows, was questioned regarding a visit Rainbow had paid to her and her husband about a month before the Gosnell murder. Objection. Sustained. Rainbow received a subpoena to appear as a witness at the first Gosnell murder trial, and defense attorney Rogers wanted to know what Rainbow said to Mrs. Crossley about the order. Objection. Sustained. Attorney Rogers then pulled out of the drawer on the trial table what looked like a small cannon and asked the witness if it was the same horse pistol Rainbow had with him at the time of his visit to the Crossley home. She said it looked the same. Objection. Sustained.

A horse pistol was typically carried in a holster on a saddle by a man who rode horseback, and the horse pistols were often issued or sold in pairs. The gun was too heavy to be carried in a holster on a man's hip.

Witness Hugh Best said he saw a wagonload of hunters go past his house the week before the murder. The hunters had dinner at the Rainbow house. Best was asked what Rainbow told him about the hunters who were taking dinner with him. Objection. Sustained.

George Yader of Long Run, the next witness to testify, had a conversation with James Gosnell a year before the murder. Gosnell told Yader that Quincy Cramblett was a nice young man. Since his son, Charles, had gotten married, Quincy was a relief. He accompanied his daughters Elva and Cora to church. He was comfortable delegating more authority to Quincy than any other young man. The witness said he heard some people laugh and make mean remarks implying that Quincy was not very smart. When he asked Gosnell about this, Gosnell said, "If anybody bought Cramblett as a fool, he was spending money very foolishly."

James Arnold was called to the witness stand. He was asked what Jeff Rainbow said in 1898 about how Gosnell would die. Objection. Sustained.

A.C. Ramsay, a hotel keeper from Adena, testified that in 1899, he was a supervisor of the district where Gosnell and Rainbow lived. He called on the men the spring before the murder. He was asked what threats Rainbow had made against Gosnell over the fence dispute. Objection. Sustained. Then Ramsay was asked what Rainbow said to him after the murder about what kind of man Gosnell was and when he ought to have died. Objection. Sustained.

Judge Hollingsworth again reminded the defense that they must show incriminating facts directly connecting Jeff Rainbow to James Gosnell's murder before any declarations could be admitted. At this time, the judge adjourned court until 1:30 p.m. on Tuesday, November 6, 1900. The witnesses were permitted to return home to vote in the presidential election.

On Tuesday, November 6, 1900, the trial resumed at 1:30 p.m., but little progress was made. The witnesses who went home to vote were unable to appear on time because the train was three hours late. The judge announced a recess at 2:30 p.m., which lasted until 4:30 p.m. The spectators waited patiently as a rumor spread that Quincy Cramblett and Jeff Rainbow may be called to the witness stand. Neither man was called. The defense recalled a few witnesses, and the questions revolved around a musket, a horse pistol, where a horse was hitched on the night of the murder and who saw Rainbow near Long Run the evening of the murder. The defense made one last effort to prove everything previously offered. The offer was refused and ruled out. Court adjourned.

When court convened on Wednesday, November 7, 1900, a new topic arose. What kind of footwear did the assassin wear? David Gotshall testified that when he saw Jeff Rainbow a short time after the murder, Jeff was wearing big rubber overshoes over heavy felt boots. Gotshall said the tracks in the garden were small with pointed toes. Sheriff Porter testified that he examined the tracks where the assassin had stood outside the window and that the tracks showed a narrow-toed shoe.

After a lunch break, a continuous stream of witnesses was recalled, including Jeff Rainbow's mother, Lavina; court stenographers; Elva and Cora Gosnell; Thomas Marchbank; William Miller; Dr. Clarence Mercer; Quincy's sister, Josie; his brother, Si; his father, John Cramblett; Dr. Barkhurst; and many others. The questions were familiar and centered on the horse pistol, the location of a musket, where a horse was hitched the night of the murder and the size of the foot tracks of the assassin.

The press recognized that much of the evidence brought out in the second trial about Jeff Rainbow's involvement could have led to his standing trial for the murder of James Gosnell. However, the repeated effort was thwarted by the court ruling that the defense had to produce incriminating evidence against Rainbow, and the defense failed.

All testimonies were completed, and each side rested its case on Wednesday afternoon, at which time, closing arguments began. State attorney John M. Cook started his closing argument late in the day but did not finish. Court adjourned. Attorney Cook concluded his closing argument at noon on Thursday, November 8.

After the lunch break, lead defense attorney, Dio Rogers, delivered his closing argument, which took most of the afternoon. Defense attorney Emmett E. Erskine began his argument but did not finish until the morning of Friday, November 9.

Prosecuting attorney Addison C. Lewis spoke the remainder of Friday and concluded his argument on Saturday, November 10, 1900. Prior to the arguments, Judge Hollingsworth instructed the attorneys to take as much time as they needed, as this was a very significant case.

10

CHARGE TO THE JURY, VERDICT

When the prosecution and defense finished their arguments, Judge Hollingsworth delivered his charge to the jury, which was long, possibly longer than the extensive orations of the attorneys. Hollingsworth reminded the jury that the indictment of first-degree murder did not create a presumption of guilt against the defendant. The defendant was to remain presumed innocent throughout the course of the trial until the state introduced proof which would overcome the presumption. He explained to the jury four possible verdicts: (1) guilty of first-degree murder; (2) guilty of second-degree murder; (3) guilty of manslaughter; or (4) not guilty as charged.

Hollingsworth further informed the jury that the state did not claim any direct evidence that Quincy Cramblett fired the shot that killed James Gosnell. Before there could be any legal conviction of the defendant in this case, the evidence had to be so convincing that it excluded all reasonable doubt of guilt from each juror's mind. Anything a juror heard about the case prior to the trial was not to influence their minds. Any information heard prior to the trial was not to be communicated to fellow jurors during deliberations.

Judge Hollingsworth spoke for about forty minutes. He instructed the jury to take the case, elect a foreman and vote their finding, either guilty or not guilty. At the judge's conclusion, around 4:00 p.m. on Saturday, November 10, the twelve men retired to the jury room to discuss, determine and vote on the future of the accused, Quincy Cramblett. For the complete text of Judge Hollingsworth's charge to the jury, see appendix C.

Members of the jury deliberated and contemplated for four hours before reaching a final verdict. Quincy Cramblett, his family and the huge crowd of spectators waited patiently and anxiously in the Jefferson County courtroom, as well as in the hallways of the courthouse. At 8:22 p.m., the jury bell finally rang, signaling a verdict had been reached. After the jury filed into the jury box, clerk Stokes called the role, and each man answered, "Present." Quincy Cramblett sat motionless, staring straight ahead, just as he had at the first trial.

Clerk Stokes then asked, "Gentlemen of the jury, have you agreed on a verdict?" Jury foreman Yeagley handed the verdict to the clerk, who, in turn, handed it to Judge Hollingsworth. He looked at it and handed it back. Stokes read, "Not guilty."

Spectators all over the courtroom who sympathized with Cramblett erupted into wild, boisterous cheers. When order was finally restored in the court, Judge Hollingsworth thanked the jury members for their patience, service and attention to the evidence during the three weeks of the trial. He continued to thank them before he discharged them. When the attendees at a play in the opera house heard the verdict, the play was stopped for the crowd to applaud.

Quincy Cramblett, now a free man, shook hands with his attorneys Dio Rogers and Emmett Erskine, the jurors and dozens of spectators who pressed forward to congratulate him. He went to get his old hat and coat, which he had worn when he entered the jail a year prior. He followed Rogers and Erskine downstairs amid the cheering crowds. The press estimated nearly five hundred people had crowded into the corridor of the Jefferson County Courthouse to see Cramblett and shake his hand. Attorney Erskine paused long enough to use the long-distance phone to notify the press of the verdict.

Once out on the street, the men proceeded to Erskine's law office. The crowd, now estimated to number one thousand, followed and cheered loudly. After reaching the second-floor law office, Erskine opened the window. Quincy stood in the window, removed his hat and bowed to the crowd below. A short time later, Cramblett proceeded to the residence of William McMillan on Court Street, where a room had been reserved for him. The verdict was undoubtedly a great relief for Quincy Cramblett and his family.

The next day, Coroner Campbell said, "I heard two drunk fellows going down Fourth Street late Saturday night cheering for Quincy Cramblett."

On Monday, November 12, 1900, Quincy Cramblett left Steubenville with his brother-in-law Addison McLain on the Wheeling and Lake Erie

Top: "Jail Register for Jefferson County," showing Quincy Cramblett's committal record for murder charges, November 10, 1900. *Youngstown Historical Center of Industry and Labor.*

Bottom: "For the Year 1900," showing November 10, Quincy Cramblett, acquitted. *Youngstown Historical Center of Industry and Labor.*

train to return home. Quincy Cramblett was pronounced innocent and could never be retried in the future.

The press believed Judge Hollingsworth's lengthy charge to the jury favored the defendant. The jury's first ballot was reportedly eight to four favoring acquittal, but after a discussion of the judge's charge, the second ballot was unanimous for acquittal. The public and press admired Judge Hollingsworth during and after the trial for his abilities as a jurist and his gentlemanly character.

Many of the attorneys around the courthouse believed Cramblett was guilty; however, the public, who read the detailed daily coverage of the trial, was inclined to champion the defendant's cause rather than accuse him. Long after the acquittal was announced, the public continued to discuss the verdict in towns throughout Jefferson County and the surrounding region.

The press generated more questions after the Cramblett acquittal. Would Cora Gosnell marry Quincy Cramblett? Would the murderer of James H. Gosnell ever be found? Would Jeff Rainbow be questioned or indicted for the murder? In time, the answer to each of the three questions ended with a resounding, "No."

The widow, Mary Gosnell, and her daughters Elva and Cora, admired and recognized for their comportment when present in the courtroom, were afraid for their lives after learning of the acquittal. Mrs. Gosnell asked the prosecutor if she could have Quincy Cramblett put under bond to keep the peace. Prosecutor Lewis said that he discharged his duty in the case and declined to take further part in it since the jury saw fit to acquit the defendant.

Jefferson County bore the complete expense of the trial, which amounted to approximately $10,000. In 2024, this would be equivalent to about $373,271.43. Because the expenses so depleted the county's funds, the county commissioners found it necessary to issue certificates-of-indebtedness until a levy of one-half mill on taxable property could be collected. If Quincy Cramblett had been convicted, the state would have paid most of the costs.

EPILOGUE

The 1899 murder of James H. Gosnell remained an unsolved crime in Jefferson County. Quincy Cramblett was acquitted of the crime after the second trial. Jeff Rainbow was never indicted, and no one else was ever questioned, arrested or indicted as a suspect in the murder. The murder case will likely never be solved after lying dormant for over a century.

The Cramblett and Gosnell families gradually moved away from their farms on Perrin Run. They relocated to different homes, towns and counties. This author talked with several descendants of the families involved in the story. Most of the descendants revealed little, if any, knowledge about the murder story. Perhaps conversations about the gruesome details were never mentioned in family circles. If descendants did not tell the story, seek out their ancestors or ask questions, they did not learn about the crime. Several of these descendants expressed a sincere interest in knowing more of the story.

Weary of city life and having spent an extended time in the Jefferson County Jail, Quincy moved to a small farm in Jefferson County around 1905. The press never forgot him and mentioned him twice in 1905. He ventured into Steubenville on occasional business and once paid a visit to his former attorney Emmett Erskine, who held steadfast to Quincy's innocence.

In 1909, Quincy met and married Nannie Caldwell, a Cambridge girl. According to the 1910 census, the newlyweds lived near Quincy's brother, Si, in Green Township, Harrison County. The couple's only child, Ralph, was born there in 1910. Nannie died in 1913, leaving Quincy with a toddler

Quincy Cramblett lived in this house at 927 Brown Street, Cambridge, Ohio, according to the 1940 census and his death certificate. *Photograph by the author.*

Cramblett's tombstone reads, "Quincy C. (1866–1947)" and his second wife, "Jennie M. (1866–1956)," Northwood Cemetery, Cambridge, Ohio. *Photograph by the author.*

DEATHS
and
FUNERALS

Quincy C. Cramblett

Quincy C. Cramblett, former tin mill employe, died Wednesday at 2:15 p.m. at his home, 927 Brown Ave., following a serious illness of one week. His health had been failing for several years. The body was removed to the Scott funeral home where it will remain for services Saturday at 1 p.m. with Rev. Lester S. Evans, of the First Presbyterian church, in charge. Interment will be in Northwood cemetery.

Mr. Cramblett was born in Jefferson county, a son of John and Mary Anne Chance Cramblett, and had been a resident of Cambridge for 30 years. His first wife, Minnie Cramblett, died in 1913 and he later married Jennie Blackburn, who survives with one son, Ralph, of the home. One brother and two sisters are deceased.

• • •

Quincy Cramblett's obituary. *From the* Cambridge Daily Jeffersonian, *April 10, 1947.*

under three years of age. Quincy and Ralph relocated to Cambridge, likely because Nannie's family lived there. He acquired employment at various jobs while he and his son, Ralph, lived in boardinghouses for a few years. (See note 53.)

On October 29, 1921, Quincy married Jennie Mae Blackburn, another Cambridge woman, who was temporarily living in West Virginia. He worked hard and lived a respectable life. Quincy died of lung cancer on April 9, 1947, at about eighty years of age. He was a retired sheet metal worker. The working conditions could have contributed to his lung ailment. His death certificate listed the informant as Ralph Cramblett and their address as 927 Brown Street, Cambridge. Jennie Blackburn Cramblett died in 1956 in Cambridge. She was interred next to Quincy and his first wife in Northwood Cemetery.

Ralph Cramblett, Quincy's son, served in the United States Navy from 1942 to 1945. He married twice but had no children. During part of his working years, he served as a clerk at the Federal Reformatory in Chillicothe, Ohio. Ralph and his second wife were interred next to his father and mother in the Northwood Cemetery.

Elva Gosnell married Halleck "Hal" Hastings in 1903. They lived on Sycamore Street in Adena and had one daughter. When this author attended Adena Elementary School, her family lived immediately next door to Hal and Elva. Cora Gosnell married George Gosnell in 1905. They also lived on Sycamore Street, two houses away from Elva. They had one son.

This author does not believe her father, Sterling Glover, knew that he, George F. Gosnell and Mary (Brown) Gosnell were second cousins and that William and Nancy Haynes Barkhurst was their common ancestral couple. The author is a third cousin to Elva and Cora. She wishes she had known these relationships when the families were her neighbors on Sycamore Street in Adena.

APPENDIX A
CHART OF FAMILY RELATIONSHIPS

Direct lineage and those involved in the story are in bold and marked with a hashtag (#). Descendant lists of siblings are marked with a plus (+). Same persons are marked with a slash (/). Asterisks mark the murder victim and the alleged shooter.

Relationships:
Line 1—siblings, sons and daughters of William Barkhurst and Nancy Haynes

Line 2—first cousins, with exceptions of Mary E. Barkhurst and Rebecca Barkhurst, who are sisters; and Margaret Ann Barkhurst and Hannah Barkhurst, who are sisters.

Line 2 to 3—first cousins once removed, with exceptions of Mary L. Brown and George F. Gosnell, who are first cousins; and Clayton Carter and Hyantha Carter, who are first cousins.

Line 3—second cousins, with exceptions of Mary L. Brown and George F. Gosnell who are first cousins, and Clayton Carter and Hyantha Carter who are first cousins.

Lines 3 to 4—second cousins once removed, with the exception of Charles, Cora and Elva, who are first cousins once removed from George F. Gosnell.

Line 4—third cousins, with the exception of Charles, Elva and Cora, who are siblings. Cora Gosnell and George F. Gosnell were married; they were first cousins once removed. Had Cora married Quincy Cramblett, their relationship would have been second cousins once removed. The author, Rena L. (Glover) Goss, is a third cousin of Charles, Elva, Cora and Ralph.

WILLIAM BARKHURST — NANCY HAYNES

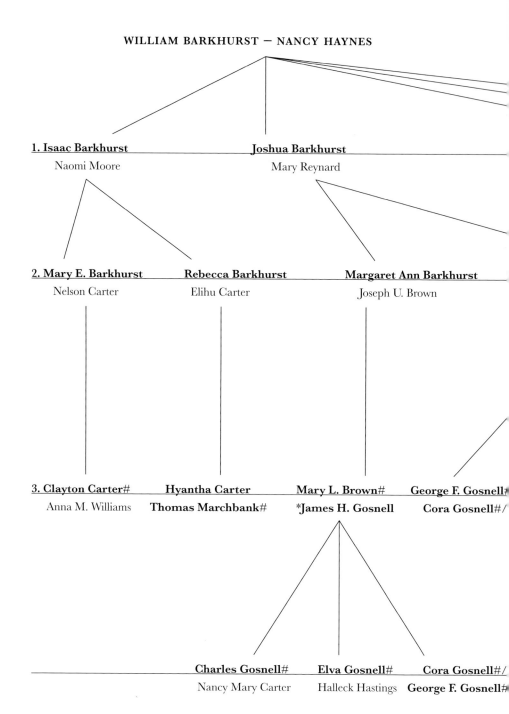

1. Isaac Barkhurst

Naomi Moore

Joshua Barkhurst

Mary Reynard

2. Mary E. Barkhurst

Nelson Carter

Rebecca Barkhurst

Elihu Carter

Margaret Ann Barkhurst

Joseph U. Brown

3. Clayton Carter#

Anna M. Williams

Hyantha Carter

Thomas Marchbank#

Mary L. Brown#

*James H. Gosnell

George F. Gosnell#

Cora Gosnell#/

Charles Gosnell#

Nancy Mary Carter

Elva Gosnell#

Halleck Hastings

Cora Gosnell#/

George F. Gosnell#

Margaret Barkhurst
James Chance

Mary Barkhurst
Josiah Glover Jr.

Jacob Barkhurst
Mary Moore

Hannah Barkhurst
Joseph Gosnell#

Mary Ann Chance#
John Cramblett#

Wm. L. Glover+
Merle Gill
Susan Glover#+
Wm. Comly
Esther Glover#+
Margaret Eliz. Glover+
Milton Hall#

Wm. B. Barkhurst
Rebecca Moore

*Quincy Cramblett+
Nannie Caldwell
Eliza Nora Cramblett#+
William Miller#
Mary Josephine Cramblett#+
Addison McClain#

Sterling Glover#+
Faye L. Grove
Harold Glover#+
Emily Ashman

Dr. S.O.Barkhurst#+
Mary Graham
Martha A.Barkhurst+
Wm. Cheffy#
Ellsworth Barkhurst#+

Ralph Cramblett

Rena L. Glover#
Larry D. Goss#

MAPS OF
JEFFERSON COUNTY

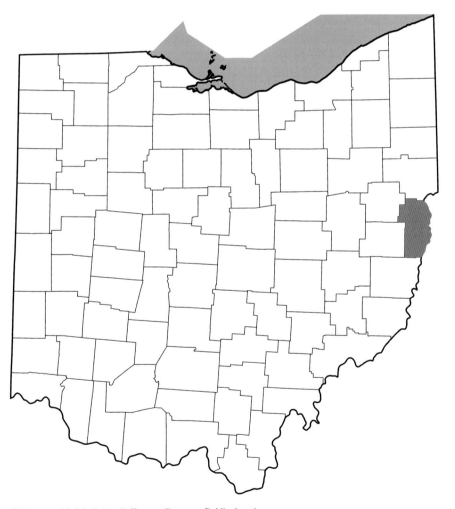

Ohio map highlighting Jefferson County. *Public domain.*

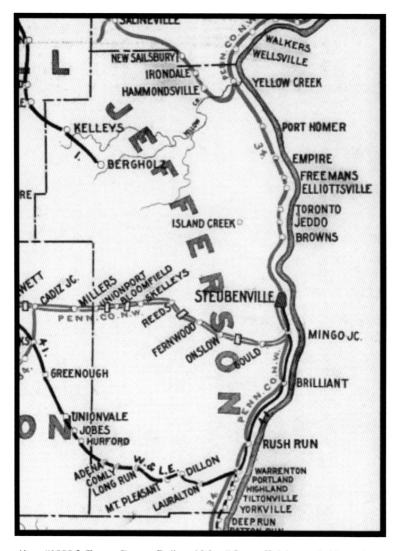

Above: "1898 Jefferson County Railroad Map." Law officials traveled by train from Steubenville to investigate the Gosnell murder and got off at Comly or Long Run Station. *Public domain.*

Opposite: A Jefferson County Township map shows towns mentioned in this book. *Public domain.*

Appendix C

JUDGE HOLLINGSWORTH'S CHARGE

On Saturday, November 10, 1900, Judge Hollingsworth made his lengthy charge to the jury and sent the twelve men on the jury out to make their determination in the second murder trial in which Quincy Cramblett was accused of first-degree murder. The verdict was reached that evening and was published in the Monday edition of the *Herald Star*, November 12, 1900. The entire unedited text of the charge appeared in the same edition on page 3. An edited version can be found in chapter 10 of this book.

> *Charge of the Court*
> *Delivered to the Jury in the Cramblett Murder Trial*
> *Judge Hollingsworth Says Mere Probability of Guilt or*
> *A Preponderance of Evidence Not Sufficient to Convict.*

> *Judge Hollingsworth's charge to the jury in the Cramblett murder trial was as follows:*

> *"Gentlemen of the Jury:*

> *"The indictment in this case charges that the defendant, Quincey [sic] Cramblett, on the 4th day of November, 1899, within the county of Jefferson, and State of Ohio, killed one James Gosnell, and charges that he thereby committed the crime of murder in the first degree. The*

indictment also contains the charges, about the same act, that it was murder in the second degree, or manslaughter. So that the questions the jury are to try and determine, are, whether the unlawful homicide was committed, and, if so who is the guilty agent, and what is the degree of the crime.

"In the investigation of every case where crime is charged, there is a positive rule of law, that should be stated by the Court, and ought to be borne in mind by the jury and that is, that the accused be presumed to be innocent. It is not thereupon that the law authorized the inquiry that was made of each of you at the impaneling of the jury, as to whether you had formed any opinion and if you had heard of the case, and formed an opinion, whether you believed you could erase that opinion entirely from your minds, as to render an impartial verdict upon the testimony wholly uninfluenced by such opinion and it was necessary that the Court should be satisfied that you could do so, because it was necessary that you should enter upon the investigation of the case with free and impartial minds, and with the presumption of innocence in favor of the prisoner. This presumption of innocence is not a mere form or shadow to be disregarded by the jury at its pleasure, but is an essential and substantial part of the law of this case. It is a legal right of the defendant and binding upon the conscience of the jury and it is the duty of the jury to give the defendant the full benefit of this presumption, and to acquit the defendant unless you feel compelled to find him guilty, as charged, in some degree, by the law and the evidence in the case convincing you of his guilt, as charged and beyond a reasonable doubt. A reasonable doubt, gentlemen, in legal procedure, is one which exists in the mind of a reasonable man, after giving full and due weight to all the evidence—both that of the State and of the defense—and such as will leave the mind in a condition in which he is not honestly satisfied and honestly convinced to a moral certainty of the guilt of the accused. It is an honest uncertainty existing in the mind of an honest, impartial and reasonable man, after a full and fair consideration of all the evidence, with a determination to ascertain the truth, regardless of consequences. Mere possibilities, or probabilities are not sufficient to warrant a conviction; neither is it sufficient that the greater weight of the evidence supports the averments of the charge; nor is it sufficient, that upon the doctrine of chances, it is more probable that the defendant is guilty; but to warrant a conviction he must be proved to be guilty, so clearly and conclusively that there is no reasonable theory upon which he may be innocent when all the evidence and facts of the case are *considered together. The finding of this indictment, by the Grand Jury, creates no presumption of guilt against the defendant; but, he is, in law, innocent, and that presumption of innocence follows him and remains and abides with him throughout the whole course of the trial until the State has introduced proof of such a character as rebuts and overcomes this presumption of innocence and has satisfied you beyond all reasonable doubt of the truth of each and all the several averments of fact in the indictment essential to constitute the crime charged against the defendant. Before a conviction can be had under this indictment there are certain essential elements of the crime charged which must be established by the State to your satisfaction and by the high degree of proof I have indicated. These essential elements of fact are: that the crime was committed by this defendant, in the County of Jefferson, and State of Ohio; that James Gosnell, named in the indictment, was a person in being; that he is now dead; that he came to his death by reason of a mortal wound inflicted upon him by this defendant, in the manner and form, with the intent and purpose, and by the means mentioned and described in the indictment. These are all essential facts to be determined by you from the evidence in the case, and if the State has failed to establish any or all of them to your satisfaction, to the extent, and in the manner I have indicated, the defendant could not and should not be convicted. While it is essential to a conviction that the jury should find with the State upon all the foregoing essential averments of fact, yet I may say, there is no serious contention between the State and the accused upon the facts, that an unlawful homicide was committed in this county, that James Gosnell is dead; but the important, pivotal and tentative question is, as to the guilty agency of this defendant, Quincey Cramblett. By his plea of not guilty, he denies his guilt, and the question of his guilt or innocence is submitted to you for your consideration and decision. There are four possible verdicts in this case, viz: Guilty of murder in the first degree as he stands charged in the indictment; guilty of murder in the second degree as he stands charged in the indictment; guilty of manslaughter as he stands charged in the indictment; or not guilty as he stands charged in the indictment. The facts of the case are for the sole and exclusive consideration of the jury, and all the Court can do is state certain general rules of law that may be found applicable to the various features of the testimony and to the questions of fact that are presented by the evidence that you have to decide, touching the several degrees of crime charged in the indictment. I will first give you what the statutes of Ohio provide shall constitute the several degrees of homicide charged by the terms of this indictment, and then call your attention to the specific terms employed by the statutes in defining the different degrees. Under the statutes of this State, murder in the first degree, so far as it is necessary for the purpose of this case, is defined as follows: Whoever, purposely and with deliberate and premeditated malice kills another is guilty of murder in the first degree. Murder in the second degree is defined as follows: Whoever, purposely and maliciously kills another is guilty of murder in the second degree. And whoever unlawfully kills another is guilty of manslaughter.*

"Before a conviction can be had under this indictment the State must have furnished evidence of such a character as to exclude every reasonable doubt of the guilt of the defendant of the crime charged and all the facts proved must be consistent with his guilt and inconsistent with his innocence, and before you will be authorized to render a verdict of guilty against the defendant in this case you must find from the evidence adduced and from the proof admitted upon the trial, that each and every fact necessary to be proven has been separately and independently established by proof that shall satisfy you with a degree or certainly exclude from your minds every other reasonable conclusion except that of the guilt of the defendant, and your minds and judgments must be so satisfied that the crime charged was committed by this defendant, and so satisfied as to have no other reasonable or rational conclusion possible from the evidence, facts and circumstances of the case, you will be justified and are required to consider a reasonable doubt as existing, if the material facts, or any one of them, without which guilt cannot be established, may be fairly and reasonably reconciled with the innocence of the defendant, and upon all doubtful questions or propositions, material and necessary to warrant conviction, the presumption of innocence which follows the defendant is sufficient, in law, to turn the scales in his favor. If you shall find the killing to have been done unlawfully and purposely, before the defendant can be convicted of the crime of murder in the first degree you must be satisfied, as stated, and further find that the same was done with deliberate and premeditated malice, and that would require you to find that he had formed the purpose to kill in his mind; that having so formed such purpose, the same was by him deliberated upon, turned over in his mind and premeditated before the act of killing was done. The law fixes no time during which such premeditation and deliberation shall take place. It is not necessary that it be of any specific length of time, but you must be satisfied from the evidence, as stated, and to the extent

stated, that the defendant had formed the purpose to kill in his mind, had deliberated upon it, and that some period of time had elapsed after the purpose was formed and before the act of killing was done. I will now define to you what is meant by the terms unlawfully, purposely *and* maliciously. Unlawfully *means to do an act prohibited by law.* Purposely, *as used in the statute defining the crime of murder, implies an act of the mind or will. It means an intention to do the act, as counter-distinguished from accident or mischance. Ordinarily the purpose to kill is to be gathered from the circumstances under which the killing is done. The presence of purpose is a question of fact to be determined by you from the evidence. The law presumes that every rational person intends the natural and probable consequences of his acts, purposely done. If you shall find from the evidence, as stated, that Quincey Cramblett intentionally did an act, the usual and natural consequences of which would be to take the life of James Gosnell then you would be justified in finding that the act was purposely done. Malice is likewise an essential element of the crime of murder in the first or second degree. The malice of homicide has been described as such a depraved condition of the mind as shows a total disregard of social and moral duty and a heart wholly bent on evil. A wanton or cruel injury to another, done without excuse or mitigation is evidence of malice. Anger or passion roused by a sudden quarrel is not malice. Passion and malice are different and inconsistent native powers.* Malice *implies a mind and under the control of reason, while passion, for the time, clouds the reason and controls and sways the action of the person under its influence. Then gentlemen if you are satisfied from all the evidence, facts and circumstances to the extent I have stated that the defendant, Quincey Cramblett, on or about Nov. 4, 1899 in this county, and State in the manner and form mentioned and described in the indictment, did unlawfully and purposely and of deliberate and premeditated malice kill James Gosnell then he is guilty of murder in the first degree under this indictment, and you should so say by your verdict, but if you entertain a reasonable doubt as to the existence of any one or all of these elements of murder in the first degree as charged, having been established by the evidence in this case, it will be your duty to acquit the defendant of the crime of murder in the first degree as therein charged.*

"If you find the defendant is not guilty of murder in the first degree, you may then inquire further and ascertain from the evidence whether under this indictment he is guilty of murder in the second degree. The essential elements of this crime are the same as murder in the first degree,

except that it is not necessary for the state to show that the killing was done of deliberate and premeditated malice. If you are satisfied beyond a reasonable doubt that the defendant, Quincey Cramblett, at the time and place aforesaid, in the manner and by the means mentioned and described in the indictment, did unlawfully, purposely and maliciously, but without deliberation and premeditation, kill James Gosnell, then he is guilty of murder in the second degree, and you should so find by your verdict. If, however, you have any reasonable doubt as to the essentials of any one or all of the elements of murder in the second degree having been established by the evidence, it will be your duty to acquit the defendant of the crime of murder in the second degree, as charged.

"In considering the evidence and determining whether or not the defendant is guilty of murder in the second degree you should apply the same definition to the words, 'that unlawfully, purposely and maliciously,' and the terms, 'malice and purpose' or any other terms therein used, as have already been given you in connection with the instructions as to murder in the first degree. The law presumes any intentional felonious killing to be murder in some degree, but this presumption rises no higher than second degree, unless the State by clear and satisfactory evidence establishes the guilt of the defendant of the higher crime to the extent, and in the manner, already stated. If you, in your investigation of this case, should find the defendant not guilty of murder in the first or second degree, you may inquire further, and determine if he is guilty of unlawfully killing James Gosnell in the manner and by the means and at the time and place charged in the indictment, and if you should be satisfied to the extent, and in the manner stated that the defendant did unlawfully kill James Gosnell, then you should find him guilty of manslaughter as he stands charged, and return a verdict accordingly; but if you are not satisfied then you should acquit the defendant. In manslaughter the unlawful killing may be without malice, either upon a sudden quarrel or intentionally, while the slayer is in the commission of some unlawful act, and the same certainty of proof is required, and the same degree of proof as indicated as being necessary in murder before a verdict of guilty can be reached against the defendant for manslaughter.

"Gentlemen, in criminal cases such as this, the evidence of the State may be either direct and positive or wholly circumstantial. It is not always possible in criminal cases to establish guilt by direct and positive evidence. Nor is it necessary that it should be, and the law provides that circumstantial evidence alone, where sufficient to satisfy the minds of the

jury, beyond all reasonable doubt, shall justify conviction. The State does not claim in this case to have any direct and positive evidence bearing upon the question that this defendant, Quincey Cramblett, fired the shot that killed James Gosnell. It is not claimed, and there is no evidence to show that any one saw the person who fired it or the weapon used, but to sustain that issue the State relies wholly upon circumstances, or a chain of circumstances, which it is claimed shows his guilt. Therefore it must be remembered by you, and you are instructed that before there can be a legal conviction of the defendant in this case, the evidence must be so clear and convincing as to exclude from your minds all reasonable doubt of the guilt of the defendant. Each and every circumstance and fact from which an inference is sought to be drawn against the defendant must be proven beyond the existence of a reasonable doubt before such inference can be drawn therefrom, and the hypothesis of guilt should flow naturally from the facts found and be consistent with them all. Before any such inference can be drawn therefrom and such fact relied upon as the basis of any legal inference against the defendant, it must be and indubitably connected with the main charge in this case, viz: The killing of James Gosnell by the defendant. If the evidence in the case can be reconciled with the innocence of the accused, you should so reconcile it. It is not sufficient, as I have said to warrant the jury in returning a verdict of guilty that the facts and circumstances established by proof coincide with, account for and therefore render probable the hypothesis of guilt, but such proof must exclude to a moral certainty every reasonable hypothesis than that of guilt. The defendant has introduced evidence as to his previous good character, which he has a right to do. It is evidence of a character tending to raise a probability, that having such a character and reputation for peace and good order, that he would not and did not commit the crime charged. It is not however, conclusive, it is simply evidence to be considered by you with all the other evidence, facts and circumstances for the purpose of determining whether the proof, taken as a whole, establishes his guilt beyond a reasonable doubt. If, notwithstanding his previous good character you are satisfied, beyond a reasonable doubt of his guilt, you should so pronounce by your verdict, only if such evidence raises a reasonable doubt in your minds as to his guilt, then you should unhesitatingly give him the benefit of the doubt and acquit him. One of the defenses interposed by the defendant in this case is what is known in law as an 'alibi,' that is, that the defendant was at another place at the time of the commission of the crime charged and therefore could not have committed it. And you are instructed gentlemen that such is a proper and legitimate defense and all the evidence bearing upon this defense should be carefully weighed and considered by the jury together with the other evidence adduced and admitted in the case. And if the jury entertains any reasonable doubt as to whether the defendant was in some other place when the crime was committed, they should give the defendant the benefit of such doubt and find him not guilty.

"Evidence has been permitted to go to the jury touching the finding of a gun or musket in the corn crib of John Cramblett, the father of the defendant and of the breaking up and hiding of the same, as well as the finding of, and the production of the broken parts of said gun in evidence. This evidence was permitted for the sole and exclusive purpose of identifying the broken parts as parts of the same gun or musket claimed by the State to have been at the Cramblett homestead, at or shortly prior to the killing of James Gosnell, and I charge you that you must not consider this evidence for any other purpose than to the extent it may aid you in determining the identity of the gun, and that for any other purpose the evidence must be wholly incomplete, it is not claimed by the State that the defendant was in any manner, directly or indirectly, connected with the finding or breaking of the gun and you should be especially guarded not to visit upon the defendant any of its consequences. Gentlemen, some questions have been asked of witnesses during the progress of the trial which were not permitted by the Court to be answered by them. The fact that questions have been asked or what such questions might imply, should not be considered by you except as they have been permitted to be answered by the witnesses. You should determine the cause and the facts necessary to be proven, to show the guilt or innocence of the defendant from the evidence which has been permitted to be given to you by the Court. You will studiously endeavor to entirely erase such questions from your minds and discuss any inferences or impressions you may have gathered there from, and also to dismiss from your consideration any statements made by counsel that have not been supported by proof. If the testimony offered in this case, and admitted by the Court, tends to show that some other person other than this defendant, killed James Gosnell and such testimony, when considered with all the other evidences, facts and circumstances is in your judgments, sufficient to and does raise a reasonable doubt as to the defendant's guilt in the minds of the jury, there and in that event you should give the prisoner the benefit of such doubt and acquit him; but you are further instructed that it is not made the duty of the jury to go outside *of the pale of the facts and circumstances proven on the trial of this case to find the slayer of James Gosnell, but only to consider the facts and circumstances offered on the trial of the case, as they may bear upon, or throw light upon the question of the guilt or innocence of this defendant."*

APPENDIX D
THE FAMILIES

In this true crime story, a large number of the family members with the surnames Barkhurst, Brown, Carter, Chance, Cramblett, Glover and Gosnell were related to and descended from William and Nancy (Haynes) Barkhurst. The living descendants seemed to know little about the relationships. The chart in appendix A shows the complicated connections within the families horizontally, vertically and diagonally. The chart, with explanations, helps clarify how everyone was related.[1]

Barkhurst was a common name in Jefferson County, Ohio, in 1900. The given names of Jacob, William, Margaret and Mary were often repeated from one generation to the next, which posed a challenge when researching early records. For example, William and Nancy Barkhurst had a daughter named Margaret. Their son Joshua named a daughter Margaret Ann, likely after his sister Margaret.

The numerous misspellings that frequently occurred in vital and census records further complicated research. Barkhurst acquired the following unique spellings: Barcus, Barkus, Barkhust, Barcust and Bencast. When William and Nancy's daughter Margaret married James Chance, her misspelled surname was clearly readable on the marriage record as Bencast. However, the index showed the correct spelling, Barkhurst.

The 1850, 1860 and 1870 census records named each member of the household and their age but did not indicate their relationship to the head of the household. The 1880 census stated each individual's relationship to the head of household. In 1900, each person's month and year of birth was stated. The census records, which did not show a relationship, were frequently proven at a later time through wills and probate records.

Marriage records were kept earlier than other vital records but often contained only the essentials, such as the names of the couple and the date and county of the marriage. But wills and probate records contained important missing information by naming heirs and their relationship to the deceased person.

When James H. Gosnell's widow, Mary (Brown) Gosnell, testified in court in 1900, Attorney Cook asked "as to what relationship existed between her and Quincy Cramblett, the defendant." Mrs. Gosnell said she "had heard it said that her grandpap and Quincy's mother's mother were brother and sister."[2] She was correct. Joshua Barkhurst, her "grandpap," and Margaret Barkhurst Chance, Quincy's grandmother, were brother and sister. Mrs. Gosnell seemed to confess that the relationship was based on hearsay.

William and **Nancy (Haynes) Barkhurst**, the ancestral couple in this story lived in Jefferson County, Ohio, for most of their lives. William was born in 1785 in Maryland according to census records.[3] He served in the War of 1812 from Jefferson County.[4] Nancy Hayne(s) was born in 1784 in Kentucky.[5] William and Nancy allegedly married in 1805, but no record of that marriage appeared in Jefferson County.[6] Nor did a record appear in other possible states, such as Maryland, West Virginia (at the time Virginia) or Kentucky. The couple had six known children who were found in Jefferson County, Ohio records, the federal census records, plus other documents and historical writings. Five of these six children had descendants directly connected to or involved in this true crime story.

Nancy's father, **Thomas Haynes**, who lived in Jefferson County, is cited here because his will named children, grandchildren and others. Nancy died in 1842, before her father. Thomas Hayne's will was dated September 11, 1844, and probated on July 29, 1845, in Jefferson County. He named in his will "daughter Nancy Barcust…and…William Barcust, husband of my daughter Nancy dec'd [deceased]." He also bequeathed money to "my three grandsons, Sons of Said Nancy Barcust dec'd to wit Isaac Barcust, Jacob Barcust, and Joshua Barcust."[7] As stated, this source proved father/daughter and grandfather/grandchild relationships.

THE SIX CHILDREN OF WILLIAM AND NANCY (HAYNES) BARKHURST

Isaac Barkhurst (1806–1893)[8] married **Naome Moore** (unknown birth and death dates) on September 1, 1825, in Jefferson County[9]; married **Isabel Moore** (circa 1806–circa 1834) on May 29, 1833, in Harrison County, Ohio[10]; married **Hannah Marshall** (1808–1886) on September 2, 1835, Jefferson County, Ohio.[11]

Jacob Barkhurst (1808/9–1881)[12] married **Mary Elenor Moore** (unknown birth date–1837) on February 25, 1830, Jefferson County, Ohio[13]; married **Jane Reynard** (circa 1813–1859) on March 20, 1841, Jefferson County, Ohio.[14]

Joshua Barkhurst (1811–1891)[15] married **Mary Reynard** (1808 or 1810–1872) on June 27, 1831, Jefferson County, Ohio[16]; married **Hannah Reynard** (circa 1825–1888) on October 15, 1873.[17]

Margaret "Peggy" Barkhurst (1813–1836)[18] married on April 30, 1829, **James Chance** (1808–1915).[19]

Mary "Polly" Barkhurst (1816–1872)[20] married on July 3, 1834, **Josiah Glover Jr.** (1814–1897).[21]

John Lessly Barkhurst (1821–1902)[22] married **Louisa Parkinson** (1814–1883) in 1844[23]; married **Sarah K. Kithcart** (1839–1929) on January 28, 1885.[24] John testified at one of the Cramblett trials, but he had no descendants who were involved in the story.

William Barkhurst's will, made in Jefferson County, Ohio, and dated April 20, 1858, explicitly named his six children, Isaac, Jacob, Joshua, Mary and John, plus two of his grandchildren, Mary Ann Chance and John M. Chance, children of his deceased daughter Margaret (Barkhurst) Chance.[25]

After William's wife, Nancy, died in 1842, he married **Isabelle (Haines/Haynes) Haymaker** on November 26, 1845, Jefferson County.[26] Isabelle was Nancy's younger sister and a widow. No children were born in the second marriage.

Five of William and Nancy's children, Isaac, Jacob, Joshua, Margaret and Mary, had descendants who had a connection to or were involved in this story through marriages into the following families: Gosnell, Brown, Cramblett, Chance, Moore, Glover, Comly and Hall. Some of the five children had multiple marriages and large families. Only the direct descendants, their spouses and children with a connection to the story are documented in this appendix.

THE GRANDCHILDREN OF WILLIAM AND NANCY (HAYNES) BARKHURST

MARY E. BARKHURST > ISAAC BARKHURST > WILLIAM AND NANCY BARKHURST
Mary E. Barkhurst (1829–1875)[27] married Nelson Carter (1820–1904) on February 28, 1849 in Jefferson County.[28]

WILLIAM B. BARKHURST > JACOB BARKHURST > WILLIAM AND NANCY BARKHURST
William B. Barkhurst (1831–1903)[29] married Rebecca Moore (1841–1928) in 1860 in Jefferson County.[30]

MARGARET ANN BARKHURST > JOSHUA BARKHURST > WILLIAM AND NANCY BARKHURST
Margaret Ann Barkhurst (1836–1876)[31] married **Joseph Updegraff Brown** (1832–1925) on December 30, 1852, in Jefferson County.[32]

HANNAH BARKHURST > JOSHUA BARKHURST > WILLIAM AND NANCY BARKHURST
Hannah Barkhurst (1839/40–unknown)[33] married **Joseph Gosnell** (1852–1907) on September 2, 1873, in Jefferson County.[34]

MARY ANN CHANCE > MARGARET BARKHURST > WILLIAM AND NANCY BARKHURST
Mary Ann Chance (1831–1900/1905)[35] married **John Cramblett** (circa 1836–1910) on February 17, 1859, in Jefferson County.[36]

SUSAN GLOVER > MARY BARKHURST > WILLIAM AND NANCY BARKHURST
Susan Glover (1838–1929)[37] married **William Comly** (1825–1897) on October 11, 1866, in Jefferson County.[38]

MARGARET ELIZABETH GLOVER > MARY BARKHURST > WILLIAM AND NANCY BARKHURST
Margaret Elizabeth Glover (1848–1912)[39] married **Milton Hall** (circa 1861–1943) on December 4, 1890, in Jefferson County.[40]

ESTHER GLOVER > MARY BARKHURST > WILLIAM AND NANCY BARKHURST
Esther Glover (1850–1924) never married.[41]

WILLIAM L. GLOVER > MARY BARKHURST > WILLIAM AND NANCY BARKHURST
William L. Glover (1860–1949)[42] married **Merle Garnet Gill** (1884–1964) on November 25, 1903, in Jefferson County.[43]

THE GREAT-GRANDCHILDREN OF WILLIAM BARKHURST AND NANCY HAYNES

THEODORE CLAYTON CARTER > MARY E. BARKHURST > ISAAC BARKHURST > WILLIAM AND NANCY BARKHURST
Theodore Clayton Carter (also known as Clayton T. Carter) (1850–1917)[44] married **Anna Margaret Williams** (1848–1887) on October 17, 1878, in Jefferson County, Ohio.[45]

SILAS OSBORN BARKHURST > WILLIAM B. BARKHURST > JACOB BARKHURST > WILLIAM AND NANCY BARKHURST
Silas Osborn Barkhurst (1863–1942)[46] married **Mary E. Graham** (1863–1934) on April 17, 1890, in Toronto, Jefferson County, Ohio.[47]

GEORGE F. GOSNELL > HANNAH BARKHURST > JOSHUA BARKHURST > WILLIAM AND NANCY BARKHURST
George F. Gosnell (1875–1951)[48] married **Cora Gosnel** (1883–1962) on January 18, 1905, in Mahoning County, Ohio.[49]

MARY L. BROWN > MARGARET ANN BARKHURST > JOSHUA BARKHURST > WILLIAM AND NANCY BARKHURST
Mary L. Brown (1855–1930)[50] married **James H. Gosnell** (1842–1899) in 1870 in Independence, Pennsylvania.[51]

QUINCY CRAMBLETT > MARY ANN CHANCE > MARGARET BARKHURST >
WILLIAM AND NANCY BARKHURST
Quincy Chance Cramblett (1867–1947)[52] married **Nannie R. Caldwell** (1883–1913) on November 17, 1909, in Cambridge, Guernsey County, Ohio[53]; married **Jennie May Blackburn** (1866–1956) on October 29, 1921, in Fairmont, Marion County, West Virginia.[54]

STERLING JOSEPH GLOVER > WILLIAM L. GLOVER > MARY BARKHURST >
WILLIAM AND NANCY BARKHURST
Sterling Joseph Glover (1906–1998)[55] married **Faye Lyda Grove** (1912–1999) on November 22, 1933, in Cadiz, Harrison County, Ohio.[56]

THE GREAT-GREAT-GRANDCHILDREN OF WILLIAM BARKHURST AND NANCY HAYNES

Having arrived at this point in the Barkhurst family's history, no descendant is alive who had actual involvement in or firsthand knowledge of the love and murder story. Sisters Elva and Cora and their spouses, siblings and their immediate descendants passed away several decades ago. This author learned of the story from ancestors who were born a few years after the event. Descendants of true crime writers have not researched the story because they lacked knowledge of the event and possibly live a great distance from Jefferson County. Some descendants have heard fragments of the event, if anything, from a previous generation. The story is over 120 years old.

ELVA GOSNELL > MARY L. BROWN > MARGARET ANN BARKHURST >
JOSHUA BARKHURST > WILLIAM AND NANCY BARKHURST
Elva Gosnell (1878–1960)[57] married **Halleck "Hal" Hastings** (1884–1952) on February 4, 1903, in Jefferson County, Ohio.[58]

CORA GOSNELL > MARY L. BROWN > MARGARET ANN BARKHURST >
JOSHUA BARKHURST > WILLIAM AND NANCY BARKHURST
Cora Gosnel [sic] (1882–1962)[59] married her first cousin once removed **George F. Gosnell** (1875–1951) on January 18, 1905, in Mahoning County, Ohio. For Cora's birth and death record, see endnote 49.

RENA GLOVER > STERLING GLOVER > WM. L. GLOVER > MARY
BARKHURST > WILLIAM AND NANCY BARKHURST
Rena Glover (1937–)[60] married **Larry Dean Goss** (1937–2019) on June
7, 1964, in Adena, Jefferson County, Ohio.[61]

THE CHANCE FAMILIES

James Chance and Margaret Barkhurst were married on April 30, 1829,
in Jefferson County, Ohio. They had two children: Mary Ann Chance and
John M. Chance. Margaret died circa 1836 around the age of twenty-
three. No records were available about Margaret's death or burial. Death
records were not mandated in Ohio at that time. Church records where
Margaret may have been a member were also not available for that time.
James and the two children were not found in any records for the next
several years.

In the 1850 census, Mary Ann Chance appeared in the household of her
maternal aunt Mary (Barkhurst) Glover and her husband, Josiah Glover,
plus the seven Glover children, Sarah A., Nancy, Susanna (Susan), George
W., Josephine, Jefferson and Margaret E. How long Mary Ann Chance lived
with the Glover family is uncertain. Josiah Glover owned a farm in Harrison
County, which happened to be adjacent to the Jefferson County farm where
his family resided. The farm in Green Township, Harrison County, was
likely the location where John and Mary Ann (Chance) Cramblett were
living during the 1860 census. It was near the Glover farm where Mary Ann
was raised and lived in 1850. By 1870, John and Mary Ann had moved to
a different location in Smithfield Township, Jefferson County. After Mary
Ann's cousin Susan Glover Comly became a widow in 1897, Susan rented
her farm to the Crambletts.

According to the oral history told by Mary (Barkhurst) Glover's
granddaughter Hilda (Glover) Palmer, Mary traveled regularly to the home
of her niece Mary Ann (Chance) Cramblett to care for her during an illness.
Mary Glover became sick, perhaps with pneumonia, and died in February
1872 at the age of fifty-five.

Josiah Glover's last will and testament was dated September 8, 1892.
Following his death in 1897, the will was read at the probate court in
Steubenville. Among the bequeaths, this was stated: "Item 3rd, I bequeath
to my niece Mary Ann Cramblet raised in my family (100) one hundred
dollars." The word *raised* suggested that Josiah and Mary likely brought

young Mary Ann Chance into their home soon after her mother, Margaret, died. Mary Ann may have been with the Glovers until she married John Cramblett in 1859.

THE CRAMBLETT FAMILIES

Like other surnames, Cramblett underwent numerous misspellings in transcriptions of census and vital records. It appeared as Cramblet, Cramlet, Bramlet and Gambeth. John Cramblett and Mary Ann Chance married in 1859 and appeared in the 1860 census living in Green Township, Harrison County. They then moved to another location in Smithfield Township, Jefferson County, and finally rented a farm on Perrin Run in Smithfield Township from Mary Ann's cousin Susan Glover Comly. By the 1900 census, John and Mary Ann Cramblett were the father-in-law and mother-in-law residing in the household of their son-in-law Addison McClain, head; daughter Josephine (likely earlier named Mary J.); and their two children, Beryl G. (female) and Howard E. (male).[62] They lived in the village of Smithfield. Surely, as the parents of Quincy, an accused murderer who, at the time, was lodged and enumerated in the Jefferson County Jail, John and Mary Ann Cramblett were emotionally drained. At the ages of sixty-four and sixty-nine, respectively, perhaps John and Mary Ann feared retribution. The entire family likely needed each other for consolation and comfort as much as the Gosnell family needed emotional support.

THE GLOVER FAMILIES

Josiah Glover died in 1897, and his wife, Mary, died in 1872. Several of the couple's children were involved in this story. As had previously been revealed in court testimony, Esther Glover procured a comforter to wrap around a gun that was taken from the Cramblett property. Margaret Elizabeth's husband, Milton Hall, forced the gun barrel of the alleged murder weapon down a well on the Glover farm, where he and Margaret lived. Susan (Glover) Comly, a widow, rented her farm to John and Mary Ann Cramblett and their children.

William L. Glover, the son of Josiah, did not live at the Glover farm according to the 1900 census.[63] He trained horses and lived independently in nearby Cadiz, Harrison County. At the age of forty, he likely had contact with family members to hear about the event. He told his children many family stories, but their recollection and retelling of this murder story provided only a basic outline and few, if any, of the abundant details contained in the newspaper accounts and online sources that were available later.

THE GOSNELL FAMILIES

The surname Gosnell acquired alternative spellings in census transcriptions and other records, which often made it difficult to locate the surname. Misspellings included Goslin, Gasnell, Gisnell, Goswold and Goswell. James Hartley Gosnell and Mary Louise (Brown) Gosnell had three children who were connected to the story. Elva M. Gosnell and Cora Maggie Gosnell were the central objects of Quincy Cramblett's affection. Charles C. Gosnell (1871–1950) testified in court and lived on a farm near his father and mother. The Jefferson County birth records for all four children confirmed James and Mary as their parents.[64] Clara D. (Gosnell) Gutshall (circa 1873–1955) was the daughter who married against her father's wishes.[65] The same four children were named in James Gosnell's letters of administration, shown in the probate records following his death in 1899.[66]

Elva and her husband, Hal, were interred close to both sets of their parents in Holmes Pioneer Cemetery near Adena. Their few descendants relocated to other areas of Ohio. Elva's sister Cora and George Gosnell were interred in Northern Cemetery in the village of Smithfield. Their only son and his wife were also buried in that cemetery.

THE RAINBOW FAMILIES

No family relationships were known to exist between the Rainbow family and the other named families. The family was included in this story due to Jeff's closeness to the crime, his residence on a neighboring farm and a strange transcription error. Rural farmers whose properties were adjacent often had disagreements over infringements of property lines, trespassing and even theft. James Gosnell and Jeff Rainbow were no different. Several disagreements between the two men were exposed during the murder investigation and court testimony. At one point in the investigations and trials, adequate motives and testimony suggested that Jefferson Rainbow was a strong suspect in the murder of his neighbor James Gosnell. To settle the long dispute, Jeff Rainbow may have taken matters into his own hands.

In the 1900 census, Jefferson Rainbow (1859–1944); his wife, Martha; their seven children, Nettie M. (fourteen), Rosa M. (thirteen), James L. (eleven), Harry R. (nine), Russel (six), Aineas (three) and Eugene C. (one); and Jeff's widowed mother, Lavina Rainbow, lived together in a house "500 yds [1,500 feet] up the road from the Gosnell's home."[67] A strange discrepancy arose in the transcribed marriage record of Jefferson Rainbow and Martha J. Norris. The original Jefferson County marriage record did not ask the race of each party. In the transcribed version, both Jefferson and Martha were listed as "black." No other Jefferson Rainbow or Martha Norris with the corresponding birth years lived in Jefferson County at that time. All other information regarding age, name and marriage date matched. Race was the only difference in the transcribed document. In seven census enumerations, between 1870 and 1940, which asked the question about race, both Jefferson and Martha were described as "white." Furthermore, Jefferson Alexander Rainbow's death certificate indicated his race as "white." While some information appearing on a death certificate can be suspect because the informant did not know the correct answer, the attending physician and undertaker had firsthand knowledge about Jefferson Rainbow's race, as both attended his body at the time of his death. Since a preponderance of information showed Jefferson and Martha Rainbow's race as "white," the error listing their race as "black" occurred only in the transcription of the marriage record.[68]

Personal Memories of the Author

For about two years, from the time I was six until I was eight, I lived with my family on Sycamore Street in Adena. Hal and Elva (Gosnell) Hastings were our next-door neighbors. George and Cora (Gosnell) Gosnell lived two houses away in the opposite direction. Elva walked down the street every morning to visit her sister Cora. She chatted regularly with my parents and other neighbors along the way. One year Elva presented me with a lovely birthday card signed Mrs. Hastings. I preserved it in a scrapbook of cards and memories. Little did I anticipate that someday I would write about the sisters and their life on Perrin Run.

Notes to Appendix D

1. See appendix A.
2. Chapter 5, "Testimony of Witnesses," Friday, April 6.
3. 1850 U.S. census, Jefferson County, Smithfield Township, Ohio, 176 (stamped), 551 (penned), dwelling 2221, family 2325, William Barkhurst; Ancestry, digital images, http://www.ancestry.com, from National Archives microfilm, publication M432_699; also, 1860 U.S. census, Jefferson County, Smithfield Township, Ohio, 24 (penned), dwelling 167, family 176, Wm. Barkhurst; Ancestry, digital images, http://www.ancestry.com, from National Archives microfilm, publication M653_993.
4. Ancestry, "War of 1812 Pension Application Files Index, 1812–1815," digital images, http://ancestry.com, William Barkhurst, from National Archives microfilm, publication War of 1812 Pension Applications, M313.
5. Birth records were not kept in Kentucky in 1784. Little is known about Nancy Haynes's birth and early life. Her father's will is the most definitive information available to connect her to a previous generation. No substantive information with cited sources has surfaced at this time regarding a mother's name.
6. No marriage record was found for William Barkhurst and Nancy Haynes in county or state records. Undocumented claims insist that the couple was married in 1805 in Jefferson County, Ohio. Early marriages were recorded as early as 1798 in Jefferson County. Pages of early records could have been lost, destroyed or somehow found unreadable.
7. Jefferson County, Ohio, record of wills, vol. 4, 117, Thomas Hayne, probate court office, Steubenville.
8. 1880 U.S. census, Jefferson County, Smithfield Township, Ohio, population schedule, Enumeration District (ED) 107, 33 (penned), 412 (stamped), dwelling 188, family 188, Isaac Barkhurst; Ancestry, digital images, http://www.ancestry.com, from National Archives microfilm, publication T9, roll 1037; also, Ancestry, "Ohio, County Death Records, 1840–2001, Jefferson County, Death Records, 1867–1908," http://www.ancestry.com, image 203, entry for Isaac Barkhurst. The 1860, 1870 and 1880 U.S. census records indicated Isaac Barkhurst's ages as fifty-four, sixty-four and seventy-four, respectively, which is consistent evidence that he was born in 1806.
9. Ancestry, "Ohio, County Marriages, 1774–1993," http://ancestry.com, Isaac Barkus and Naome Moore (1825). No birth or death dates were

found for Naome Moore. She likely died before 1833, as Isaac Barkhurst married a second time in 1833.

10. Ancestry, "Ohio, County Marriages, 1789–2013," http://ancestry.com, Isaac Barkhurst and Isabel Moore. No birth or death records were found for Isabel. Since Isaac Barkhurst married again in 1835, it is likely that Isabel died prior to Isaac's third marriage in 1835.

11. Ancestry, "Ohio, County Marriages, 1774–1993," http://ancestry.com, Isaac Barcus and Hannah Marshall; also, 1850 U.S. census, Smithfield Township, dwelling 2203, family 2307, Isaac Barkhurst; Ancestry, digital images, http://www.ancestry.com, from National Archives microfilm, publication M432_699, 174B, image 655. The 1850 census was the first to name all members of a household. Living in the Isaac Barkhurst residence was Hannah, who is likely the Hannah Marshall Isaac married in 1835. Also listed is Deborah, age sixteen (which indicated birth in 1834), likely the daughter of Isaac's second wife, Isabel. The remaining six children were to be born after Isaac's 1835 marriage to Hannah Marshall.

12. 1850 U.S. census, Jefferson County, Smithfield Township, Ohio, 173B and 174A (stamped), dwelling 2188, family 2292, Jacob Barkhurst; Ancestry, digital images, http://www.ancestry.com, from National Archives microfilm, M432_699. In 1850, Jacob, age forty-one; Jane, thirty-seven; William, nineteen; and Naomi, eighteen, were enumerated. In the 1860, 1870 and 1880 census records, Jacob's age was consistently correct for a birth year of 1809. Leila S. Francy, compiler, and Reva Ashcraft and Leila Francy, copiers, "Deaths Recorded in Jefferson County, Ohio 1867–1887," 1985, 8, entry for Jacob Barkhurst, Jefferson County Genealogical Society, Stratton, Ohio. Jacob Barkhurst died on August 21, 1881. Also, a tombstone inscription (Rehobeth Cemetery, near Adena, Ohio) copied by and in the possession of the author bears the same information.

13. There is no record of birth or death for Mary Elenor Moore. She likely died prior to 1841, the year Jacob married Jane Reynard. Ancestry, "Ohio County Marriages, 1774–1993," http://www.ancestry.com, Jacob Barkhurst and Mary Elenor Moore. Two children, aged nineteen and eighteen, were enumerated in the 1850 census. Mary Elenor was likely their mother.

14. The only evidence of birth and death dates for Jane appeared on the shared tombstone of her and her husband, Jacob, located in Rehobeth Cemetery near Adena: "d. Sept. 25, 1859, 46y 5m 24d," indicated

a birth date in April 1813. Also, Ancestry, "Ohio County Marriages, 1774–1993," http://www.ancestry.com, Jacob Barkhurst and Jane Reynard.

15. 1880 U.S. census, Jefferson County, Smithfield Township, Ohio, Enumeration District (ED) 107, 34 (penned), dwelling 197, family 197, Joshua Barkhurst; Ancestry, digital images, http://www.ancestry.com; Family History Film: 1255037, 412B, National Archives microfilm, publication T9. The 1880, 1870 and 1860 census records give Joshua's ages as sixty-eight, fifty-eight and forty-eight, respectively, and all three enumerations were taken in June. Joshua's alleged birthday was July 13, 1811, and perhaps the census was conducted close enough to his birthdate to accept his upcoming age. The 1850 census was taken in October, and Joshua's age was recorded as thirty-nine, which suggests an 1811 birth year. Jefferson County, probate file 5810, box 60; an application for letters of administration stated Joshua Barkhurst died "on or about 24th day of March A.D. 1891." Original early probate packets are housed at the Jefferson County Genealogical Society Office in Stratton, Ohio.

16. Mary's alleged year of birth was 1808. This author read Mary's tombstone inscription in 1961 and calculated her birth date as January 13, 1808. The 1860 and 1870 census records showed her ages as fifty-two and sixty-two, respectively, which correlated with a birth year of 1808. The 1850 census, taken in October, recorded her age as forty-four. *History of the Upper Ohio Valley*, 2 vols. (Madison, WI: Brant & Fuller, 1890), 2:207. In this history, Mary Reynard Barkhurst's year of birth is stated as 1810 and not in agreement with the 1808 date. Family Search, "Ohio County Marriages, 1789–2013," https://familysearch.org, image 648.

17. Find A Grave, "Hannah Reynard Barkhurst (1825–1888)," https://www.findagrave.com/memorial/77630981/hannah-barkhurst. Hannah Reynard's alleged birth year was 1825. Also, in the 1880 census, Hannah was recorded as being fifty-five years of age, which confirmed a birth year of 1825, and the wife of Joshua Barkhurst. The other census records showed her age as 1850, age twenty-six; 1860, thirty-six; and 1870, age forty-eight, and she was recorded as living in the household of Marmaduke and Mary Reynard, likely her parents. Hannah's death occurred in 1888. Also, Leila Francey and Reva Ashcraft, "Deaths Recorded in Jefferson County Ohio 1867–1887," 7. "Barkhurst, Hannah, born Smithfield, died there 19 June 1888." Additionally, the application for letters of administration, completed following Joshua's

death in 1891, stated the fact that he "died leaving no widow." Also, Ancestry, "Ohio County Marriages, 1774–1993," image 204, www. ancestry.com.

18. 1830 U.S. census, Smithfield, Jefferson County, Ohio, 134 (penned), James Chance; Ancestry, http://www.ancestry.com; National Archives microfilm, publication M19, roll 134. Only one female "of 15 and under twenty" was counted, likely Margaret. She was likely born around 1813, because she was the fourth of six children, with the older sibling's estimated birth years being 1806, 1808 and 1811, and the sixth child, Mary, was born in 1814, thus leaving a space between 1811 and 1814 for Margaret's birth. Margaret's death date is not exact; 1836 has been estimated. No burial location or cemetery listing for Margaret has been found. She did not appear in the 1850 census.

19. 1830 U.S. census, Smithfield, Jefferson County, Smithfield Township, Ohio, population schedule, 134 (penned), James Chance. James was likely the one male "20 thru 29" present. This would place his year of birth between 1801 and 1810. Also, "Jefferson Co., Ohio, Marriage Certificates No. 3," James Chance and Margaret Bencast, Probate Court, Steubenville. "Bencast" was apparently a misspelling for Barkhurst. Also, Ancestry, "Ohio County Marriages, 1774–1993," http://www.ancestry.com, images 6 and 267. Image 6 was a list of names of the groom and bride, plus the page number where the record was located. Margaret's surname was spelled "Bencast." However, in image 267, which was a list of the date of marriage, names of both parties, followed by an ascending number, this list stated, "1829 April 29, James Chance and Margaret Barkhurst 5593." The handwriting on all three pages was different. However, image 6 and the certificate contain the same error. After Margaret died, allegedly in 1836, a James Chance was listed in the Jefferson County records as having married a Sarah Goodwin, but after researching that family, it appeared unlikely that this was the James Chance who was married to Margaret Barkhurst Chance. James was not recognizable in any subsequent census record. No specific knowledge was evident of where he or the two children went at the exact time of Margaret's death in 1836.

20. Joel Glover, "Record and Chronology of the Origin of the Glover Family," unpublished bound record book, 1878, 10. Mary Barkhurst's birthdate was listed as August 29, 1816. Joel was Mary's brother-in-law. Also, Francy and Ashcraft, "Deaths Recorded in Jefferson County 1867–1887," 70. Mary Barkhurst Glover died on February 10, 1872.

21. Glover, "Origin of the Glover Family," 3. Josias (or Josiah) was born "November 13, 1814." Also, Francy and Ashcraft, "Deaths Recorded in Jefferson County 1867–1887," 58. "Josiah Glover, 7 May 1897." Also, "Jefferson County, Ohio, Marriage Records," 4:114, Josias Glover and Mary Barkhurst, Probate Court, Steubenville.

22. 1900 U.S. census, Jefferson County, Smithfield Township, Ohio, population schedule, Enumeration District (ED) 68, sheet 58B, dwelling 177, family 187, John L. Barkhurst; Ancestry, http://www.ancestry.com; FHL microfilm: 1241289, National Archives microfilm, publication T623. In this census, John L. Barkhurst reported his birth month and year as "Oct. 1821," and in the 1860 census, his age was recorded as thirty-nine, which is consistent with his age in the 1900 census. Death records were not required by the State of Ohio until 1908. In the application for letters of administration, which is a sworn statement, "John L. Barkhurst...died on or about 7 July 1902."

23. 1880 U.S. census, Jefferson County Ohio, Mt. Pleasant Township, population schedule, Enumeration District (ED) 103, 8 (penned), dwelling 72, family 76, John L. Barkhurst, digital image 7; Ancestry, http://www.ancestry.com; Family History film 1255037, roll 1037, National Archives microfilm T9. In the census records, Louisa's age was recorded as sixty-six in 1880, fifty-six in 1870, forty-six in 1860 and thirty-six in 1850, all consistent with a birth year of 1814. Also, Francy and Ashcraft, "Deaths Recorded in Jefferson County 1867–1887," 8, Louisa Barkhurst, April 28, 1883; Ancestry, "Ohio, County Marriages, 1789–2013, Jefferson, marriage records 1841–1850, vol. 6," http://www.ancestry.com, John Barkhurst and Louisa Parkinson.

24. 1900 U.S. census, Jefferson County, Ohio, Mt. Pleasant Township, population schedule, Enumeration District (ED) 68, sheet 58-B, dwelling 177, family 187, Sarah K. Barkhurst. Sarah stated in this census record that she was born January 1839 and her age at her last birthday was sixty-one. Also, Ancestry, "Ohio, Deaths, 1908–1932, 1938–2007," http://www.ancestry.com, entry for Sarah K. Barkhurst, 28 May 1929, citing Ohio Department of Health, Vital Statistics Unit, Columbus, OH; Ancestry, "Ohio. County Marriages, 1774–1993, Jefferson Co.," http://www.ancestry.com, John L. Barkhurst and Sarah Kithcart, certificate number 17914, 61, image 500, married January 28, 1885.

25. Jefferson County, Ohio, record of wills, 6:180, William Barkhurst, Probate Court Office, Steubenville.

26. Birth records were not kept in Ohio until 1867. In the previously cited 1850 U.S. census, Isabella was the wife of William Barkhurst, and her age was given as forty-eight, which is fairly consistent with her alleged 1800 birth date and was the best possible record. Also, Find A Grave, "Memorial 40552416," www.findagrave.com, Highland Cemetery, Mt. Pleasant, Jefferson County, Ohio; Isabella Haines Haymaker Barkhurst and first husband, John Haymaker, were buried in this cemetery, but no photographs of the tombstones are available. Also, Jefferson County, Ohio, marriage records, 1838–1866, 92, William Barkhurst and Isabella Haymaker, November 26, 1845, probate court, Steubenville.

27. 1850 U.S. census, Jefferson County, Ohio, Smithfield Township, 174 (stamped), dwelling 2191, family 2295, Mary Carter; Ancestry, http://www.ancestry.com; National Archives microfilm, roll M432_699, image 654. Mary Carter's age was listed as twenty, suggesting a birth year of 1830. The 1860 and 1870 censuses were consistent with the respective recorded ages of thirty and forty. Her tombstone shows her birth year as 1829, which could be correct, depending on how individuals calculated their age. The three censuses were taken in June and October. A tombstone photograph in possession of this author shows her birth and death dates as 1829 and 1875. Also, Family Search, "Ohio County Death Records, 1840–2001," www.familysearch.org; Jefferson, death records 1867–1908, 1:1A, image 90 of 488, county courthouses, Ohio. Mary E. Carter died on May 11, 1875.

28. 1900 U.S. census, Jefferson County, Ohio, Mt. Pleasant Township, Enumeration District (ED) 68, 92A (stamped), dwelling 463, family 492, Nelson Carter; FHL microfilm 1241289; Ancestry, www.ancestry.com. Nelson Carter's birth was given as December 1820. Also, no official death record was available in Ohio. A photograph of Nelson Carter's tombstone in the possession of this author shows his birth date as 1820 and death date as 1904. The stone is located in Holmes Pioneer Cemetery, near Adena, Jefferson County, Ohio. Also, Family Search, "Ohio County Marriages, 1789–2013," www.familysearch.org; Jefferson Marriage Records 1841–1850, 6:314, image 186, county courthouses, Ohio.

29. 1850 U.S. census, Jefferson County, Ohio, Smithfield Township, 347 (penned), dwelling 2188, family 2292, William Barkhurst; Ancestry, http://www.ancestry.com; National Archives microfilm, roll 432_699. William's age was nineteen. In the census records, his age was recorded as twenty-nine in 1860, thirty-nine in 1870, forty-nine in 1880 and sixty-eight in 1900. He gave his birth date as January 1831, which is likely his

exact birth month and year. Also, *History of the Upper Ohio Valley*, 2:172. The birth record in this text was consistent with the census birth year and included the entire date, January 27, 1831. Also, Ohio wills and probate packets, 1786–1998, Jefferson County, probate case file 8425, William B. Barkhurst (1903), application for letters of administration, August 15, 1903. The application is page 2 of the administration papers. This document states William B. Barkhurst's "on or about" death date as July 21, 1903, and names one of his sons, S. Osborne Barkhurst.

30. 1860 U.S. census, Jefferson County, Ohio, Smithfield Township, population schedule, 175 (stamped), dwelling 230, family 240, Jacob Barkhurst. Rebecca was listed as aged nineteen in 1860, twenty-nine in 1870, thirty-nine in 1880 and fifty-nine in 1900, with her birth date given as March 1841. Also, Find a Grave, "Memorial #142039164, Rebecca Moore Barkhurst, Birth: Mar. 24, 1841, Death: Nov. 24, 1928," www.findagrave.com; Family Search, "Ohio Deaths, 1908–1953," https://familysearch.org, image 2439; Ancestry, "Ohio, County Marriages, 1774–1993," http://www.ancestry.com, William Barkhurst and Rebecca Moore, January 5, 1860.

31. 1850 U.S. census, Jefferson County, Ohio, Smithfield Township, population schedule, 347 (penned), 347 (stamped), dwelling 2189, family 2293. Margaret Barkhurst was listed in the household of Joshua Barkhurst. Ancestry, http://www.ancestry.com; National Archives microfilm publication, roll M432_699. Margaret's age in this census was listed as fifteen. Her age in the 1860 census was listed as twenty-three, and in 1870, it was listed as thirty-three. Her estimated and likely birth year was 1836. Also, Family Search, "Ohio, County Death Records, 1840–2001," https://familysearch.org, Margaret A. Brown, June 26, 1876, died, FHL microfilm 900,038.

32. 1860 U.S. census, Jefferson County, Ohio, Smithfield Township, population schedule, 169 (stamped), dwelling 147, family 156, Joseph Brown; Ancestry, http://www.ancestry.com; FHL Film: 803993, National Archives microfilm publication M653. Joseph Brown's age was listed as twenty-eight in 1860. In the 1850 census, his age was listed as eighteen, and it was listed as thirty-eight in 1870, all consistent with his birth year of 1832. Also, Find a Grave, "Memorial #18802402, Burlingame City Cemetery, Burlingame, Osage Co., Kansas," www.findagrave.com. A digital image of the tombstone states the birth date as "Nov. 25, 1831." Joseph Brown's death date stated on the tombstone is "Nov. 6, 1925." Also, Ancestry, "Ohio, County

Marriages, 1774–1993," www.ancestry.com, Joseph W. Brown and
Margaret Ann Barkhurst, December 30, 1852. Margaret married at
either age fifteen or seventeen, and either was possible. See endnote 31
for her ages in the census records.

33. 1850 U.S. census, Jefferson County, Ohio, Smithfield Township,
population schedule, 347 (penned), dwelling 2189, family 2293. Hannah
Barkhurst is listed in the household of Joshua Barkhurst. Hannah's age
was listed as being eleven in 1850, twenty in 1860, thirty in 1870 and
thirty-eight in 1880. Birth records were not mandated until 1867 in
Ohio. The 1850 census was enumerated in October, so if her birthday
fell in a previous month, she could have already turned eleven. The
censuses in 1860, 1870 and 1880 were enumerated in June. The 1850,
1860 and 1870 records suggested a birth year of 1840. Her age in 1880
was not explainable. Also, no date was available for Hannah Barkhurst
Gosnell's death, which occurred sometime after the 1880 census was
taken but before her husband's death in 1907. Numerous online sites
were searched, as were printed collections of death records. The few
family trees that were posted online showed no date for her death.

34. 1860 U.S. census, Jefferson County, Ohio, Smithfield Township,
population schedule, 170 (stamped), dwelling 160, family 169. Joseph
Gosnell is listed in the household of Gideon Gosnell. In the 1860 census,
Joseph was listed as being eight years old; he was listed as eighteen in
1870, twenty-nine in 1880 and forty-seven in 1900. Most of his ages in
the census records suggest a birth year of 1852. Also, Family Search,
"Ohio, County Death Records, 1840–2001," www.familysearch.com;
Jefferson County, death records, 1867–1908, vol. 1-1A, image 470.
Joseph Gosnell died on July 28, 1907. Also, Jefferson County, Ohio,
marriage record book 8, 1866–1883, 362:14167, Joseph Gosnell and
Hannah Barkhurst, September 2, 1873, probate court, Steubenville. The
couple was married "at the residence of Joshua Barkhurst."

35. 1850 U.S. census, Jefferson County, Ohio, Smithfield Township,
population schedule, 338 (penned), dwelling 2131, family 2234. Mary
Ann Chance (age nineteen) was recorded as living in the household
of Josiah Glover. Ancestry, http://ancestry.com; National Archives
microfilm, publication M32, image 645. Also, Josiah Glover's will and
probate stated that Mary Ann Chance was raised in his family. Mary
Ann's ages are consistent throughout the census records. She was listed
in 1860 aged twenty-nine, thirty-nine in 1870, forty-nine in 1880 and
sixty-nine in 1900. Her birthdate was recorded as "May 1831." Also,

no death or burial records were available for Mary Ann Cramblett. The online Ohio Death Record Index contains no listing for her. Her husband, John Cramblett, died in 1910, according to a front page article in the *Herald Star* regarding his death in the county home. It stated that his wife died "several years earlier." This narrows the time of her death to sometime between 1900 and 1910. In 1905, when Quincy Cramblett was mentioned as visiting Steubenville, the article stated that he had lost his mother a short time before, narrowing her death date from 1900 to 1905.

36. 1850 U.S. census, Jefferson County, Ohio, Smithfield Township, population schedule, 362 (penned), dwelling 2288, family 2393. John Cramblet (age thirteen) was recorded as living in the household of Silas Cramblet; Ancestry, http://www.ancestry.com; National Archives microfilm, publication M32. In the succeeding census records, John's ages were shown as twenty-three in 1860, thirty-three in 1870, forty-four in 1880 and sixty-four in 1900, with his birthdate recorded as "April 1836." Also, the *Herald Star* published on Tuesday, August 10, 1910, that his death occurred on Sunday, August 8, 1910, and that he was over eighty years old, confirming his birth year of 1836. Also, Jefferson County, marriage record book 7, 1850–1866, 388: 10061, John Cramblet and Mary Ann Chance, February 17, 1859, probate court, Steubenville.

37. 1850 U.S. census, Jefferson County, Ohio, population schedule, 338 (penned), dwelling 2131, family 2234. Susanna (Susan) was recorded as living in the household of Josiah Glover. Susan was age eleven. Also, Glover, "Origin of the Glover Family," 10. "Susan Glover born Aug 14 1838." Also, Ohio Department of Health, death certificate, vol. 6116, certificate 65128 (1929), Susan Glover Comly, Ohio Death Certificate Index, Ohio Historical Society. Susan died on October 12, 1929.

38. 1850 U.S. census, Jefferson County, Ohio, Smithfield Township, population schedule, 345 (penned), dwelling 2175, family 2279. William Comly was recorded as living in the household of David Comly; Ancestry, http://www.ancestry.com; National Archives microfilm, publication M432. William Comly appeared at age twenty-four, living with his family. In 1860, his age was recorded as being aged thirty-three, forty-four in 1870 and fifty-four in 1880. Also, his birth likely occurred in October 1825. Also, Francy and Ashcraft, "Deaths Recorded in Jefferson County, 1888–1898," 31, record for "William Comley, died 21 Oct. 1897, age 72 yrs"; Jefferson County, Ohio, marriage record book 8,

1866–1883, 39:11939, William Comly and Susan Glover, October 11, 1866, probate court, Steubenville.

39. 1850 U.S. census, Jefferson County, Ohio, Smithfield Township, population schedule, 338 (penned), dwelling 2131, family 2234. Margaret E. was recorded as living in the household of Josiah Glover. Margaret Elizabeth Glover was age three. In 1860, she was twelve, twenty-two in 1870, thirty-two in 1880, fifty-two in 1900 and fifty-eight in 1910, the latter of which is inconsistent with the ages in previous census records. Also, Glover, "Origin of the Glover Family," 10. "Margarette E. Glover born Jan 3 - 1848." Also, Ohio Department of Health, "Ohio Deaths, 1908–1932, 1938–1944, and 1958–2007." Ancestry, "Record for Margaret Elizabeth Hall, 15 April 1912," http://www.ancestry.com.

40. 1870 U.S. census, Athens County, Ohio, Carthage Township, population schedule, 121 (stamped), dwelling 149, family 145. Henry M. (Milton) Hall was recorded as living in the household of Elisha Hall; Ancestry, http://www.ancestry.com; FHL film 552670, National Archives microfilm, publication T132. Henry Milton was age four, indicating 1866 as his birth year. The remainder of his ages recorded in the census records of 1880, 1900, 1910, 1920, 1930 and 1940 were not consistent. He could theoretically have been born between 1865 and 1870. Also, Family Search, "Ohio Death Index, 1908–1932, 1938–1944, and 1958–2007," https://familysearch.org; Ohio Department of Health, Milton Hall, 29 May 1943, Jefferson County, Ohio; Jefferson County, Ohio, marriage record book 12 (1889–1893), 225:20032, Milton Hall and Margaret E. Glover, December 4, 1890.

41. 1860 U.S. census, Jefferson County, Ohio, Smithfield Township, population schedule, 180 (stamped), dwelling 297, family 310. Esther was recorded as living in the household of Josiah Glover; Ancestry, http://www.ancestry.com; FHL Film: 803993, National Archives microfilm publication M653. Esther's age was recorded as nine. In 1870, her age was recorded as nineteen, twenty-nine in 1880 and forty-nine in 1900, and she gave her birth date as August 1850. In 1910, her age was recorded as fifty. Also, Glover, "Origin of the Glover Family," 10. "Esther Glover was born Aug 7, 1850." Also, none of the several databases for deaths on either Ancestry or Family Search showed a death record for Esther Glover. Find a Grave, "Memorial 125298815," www.findagrave.com; Cadiz Union Cemetery, Cadiz, Ohio, creator: Names in Stone, "Esther Glover d. Mar. 6, 1924"; *Cadiz*

Republican, "Esther Glover," March 13, 1924, 2, column 3, microfilm Jan. 5,1922 through Dec. 25, 1924, box 55, Puskarich Public Library, Cadiz, Ohio.

42. 1860 U.S. census, Jefferson County, Ohio, Smithfield Township, population schedule, 180 (stamped), dwelling 297, family 310; Ancestry, http://www.ancestry.com. Wm. L. was recorded as living in the household of Josiah Glover. Roll M653, FHL Film 803993, NARA microfilm publication M653; Glover, "Origin of the Glover Family," 10. "William L. Glover born January 16, 1860"; "Harrison Co., Ohio, Notebook of Marriages, Wills, Births, Deaths," section 1949: 58, William Leslie Glover, date of death, April 20, 1949, probate court, Cadiz, citing Ohio Department of Health.

43. Jefferson County, Ohio, "Births, Vol. G, 1867-1885," no. 716, 184, 11452, Myrtle Gill (also known as Merle), birth date July 29, 1884, father, Joseph Gill, mother, Levena Owens, probate court, Steubeville; Harrison County, Ohio, "Death Records 1960-61-62-63-64," 1964 section, 26, certificate of death for Merle Glover, July 28, 1964, probate court, Cadiz, Jefferson County, Ohio; "Marriage Record 17," 600, no. 27701, marriage certificate for William L. Glover and Myrtle Gill, 25 Nov. 1903, probate court, Steubenville.

44. 1850 U.S. census, Jefferson County, Ohio, Smithfield Township, population schedule, 174 (printed), dwelling 2191, family 2295. Theodore Carter was recorded as living in the household of Nelson Carter; Ancestry, http://www.ancestry.com; microfilm roll: M432_699; "Ohio, U.S., Death Records, 1908–1932, 1938–2018," Clayton Carter (also known as Theodore), Ohio Death Index, vol. 2273, certificate no. 34098, date of death 5-13-1917, 1284, image 447; Ohio Department of Health, Division of Vital Statistics, Columbus, Ohio.

45. 1850 U.S. census, Jefferson County, Ohio, Wayne Township, population schedule, 144A (printed), dwelling 2070, family 2172. Anna M. Williams, age three, was recorded as living in the household of William O. Williams; Ancestry, http://www.ancestry.com; microfilm roll: M432_699. Also, A death record is not available, except for the tombstone located in Holmes Pioneer Cemetery, near Adena, Ohio, which shows the death date as 1917 and also corroborates the birth year of 1848; a photograph of the grave stone is in the possession of this author. Also, Ancestry, "Ohio County Marriage Records, 1774–1993," http://www.ancestry.com, Jefferson, 1865–1892, digital images, 600, image 320, film number: 000900071.

46. 1870 U.S. census, Jefferson County, Ohio, Smithfield Township, population schedule, 447 (stamped), dwelling 87, family 85. Silas O. was recorded as living in the household of William Barkhurst. Ancestry, http://www.ancestry.com; roll M593, FHL Film: 552726, National Archives microfilm publication T132. Silas was recorded as aged six. In 1880, his age was listed as sixteen and thirty-six in 1900, forty-six in 1910, fifty-six in 1920, sixty-six in 1930 and seventy-six in 1940, and his birth date was given as August 1863. A birth year of 1863 appears to be correct because he gave his precise age at each census in June, not the age he would be in two months. Also, *Herald Star*, "Dr. Barkhurst Taken by Death," October 24, 1942, 7, column 5, Box F4, Schiappa Library, Steubenville. The obituary stated that Silas was seventy-nine years old on August 20, 1942, meaning his birth date was August 20, 1863. Also, Ohio Department of Health, death certificate 62424 (1942), Osborne Barkhurst, Division of Vital Statistics, Columbus. The death certificate indicated that S. Osborne Barkhurst died in the Massillon State Hospital in Massillon, Stark County, Ohio, on October 23, 1942.

47. 1870 U.S. census, Jefferson County, Ohio, Smithfield Township, population schedule, 449 (stamped), dwelling 111, family 109. Mary E. Graham was recorded as living in the household of Thomas Hamilton. Ancestry, http://www.ancestry.com; roll: M593, FHL Film: 552726, National Archives microfilm, publication T132. Mary E. Graham was listed as being seven years of age, born 1863. In the 1900 census, Mary gave her birth date as "July 1863." Also, Ohio Department of Health, death certificate 3836 (1934), Mary E. Barkhurst; Family Search, https://familysearch.org; Division of Vital Statistics, Columbus, image 917. Mary E. (Graham) Barkhurst died at age seventy. Also, "Ohio, County Marriages, 1774–1993," record for S. Osborne Barkhurst and Mary E. Graham, 17 April 1890; Ancestry, "Ohio Marriages," http://www.ancestry.com.

48. Family Search, "Ohio, County Births, 1841–2003," https://www.familysearch.org, Jefferson, image 182, county courthouses, Ohio. George F. Gosnell was born on June 29, 1875, to Jos. Gosnell and Hannah Barkhurst. Family Search, "Ohio, County Death Records, 1840–2001," https://familysearch.org, George F. Gosnell, 20 May 1951; Martin's Ferry, Belmont, Ohio, county courthouses, Ohio, FHL microfilm 2,115,367.

49. Family Search, "Ohio, County Births, 1841–2003," https://familysearch.org, Jefferson, image 115; county courthouses, Ohio. Cora

Gosnell was born on August 7, 1882. Also, Family Search, "Ohio Death Index, 1908–1932, 1938–1944, and 1958–2007," https://familysearch. org, vol. 16908, certificate number 37359, Ohio Historical Society, Columbus, Ohio. Cora Gosnell died on May 17, 1962. Also, Ancestry, "Ohio Department of Health, State Vital Statistics Unit, Columbus, Ohio, County Marriages, 1774–1993," https://ancestry.com; marriage records, Ohio marriages, Cora Gosnell and George Gosnell, 18 Jan. 1905, Mahoning County, Ohio.

50. 1860 U.S. census, Jefferson County, Ohio, Smithfield Township, population schedule, 169 (stamped), dwelling 147, family 157. Mary L. Brown, age five, was recorded as living in the household of Joseph Brown. Family Search, https://familysearch.org, image 21, citing National Archives microfilm, publication M653. No birth record was found for Mary Louise Brown. This record was the closest to prove her birth year as 1855. Also, Find a Grave, "Memorial #149112360," www.findagrave.com, data for Mary L. Gosnell (1855–1930); Holmes Pioneer Cemetery, Adena, Jefferson County, Ohio. Mary died on July 30, 1930, according to her tombstone. All death record collections on FamilySearch.org and Ancestry.com were searched with no record of Mary L. Gosnell's death.

51. Find a Grave, "James H. Gosnell (1842–1899), Memorial #149112205," www.findagrave.com. This was the only reasonable information found on James H. Gosnell's birth information. The date was "Jan. 8, 1842." Ages given in the 1850, 1860, 1870 and 1880 censuses alluded to different birth years. No birth record law was passed in Ohio until 1867. Also, Family Search, "Ohio, County Death Records, 1840–2001," https://familysearch.org, James Gosnell, 4 November 1899; death records, Smithfield Township, Jefferson, Ohio, source ID, vol. 2, 382, county courthouses, Ohio; FHL microfilm 900,038. Also, the marriage record for James H. Gosnell and Mary Louise Brown was a handwritten document signed by S.L. Davis, a minister of the gospel. The marriage between James H. Gosnell of Mt. Pleasant, Jefferson County, Ohio, and Mary L. Brown of the same place was performed on November 27, 1870, in Independence, Pennsylvania. Ray and Janet Gosnell of Reynoldsburg, Ohio, possess the original copy.

52. 1870 U.S. census, Jefferson County, Ohio, Smithfield Township, population schedule, 453 (stamped), dwelling 169, family 166. Quincy Cramlet (mispelling in census) was recorded as living in the household of John Cramlet [*sic*]. Ancestry, http://ancestry.com, image 36, FHL film

552726, National Archives microfilm, publication T132. Each of the census records correlated with a birth year of 1867. In the 1900 census, Quincy gave his birth date as March 1867.

53. 1900 U.S. census, Guernsey County, Ohio, Cambridge Township, population schedule, Enumeration District (ED) 3, 2112 and 2113 (penned), 18A and 18B (stamped), dwelling 334, family 334. Nannie B. Caldwell was recorded as living in the household of James T. Caldwell; Ancestry, http://ancestry.com; Roll 1273, FHL microfilm 1241273, National Archives microfilm, roll T623. Lacking a birth record, this census was the first in which Nannie was enumerated. It showed her age as seventeen and provided her birth month and year, February 1883.

54. 1870 U.S. census, Cambridge, Ohio, Guernsey County, population schedule, dwelling 371, family 386. Jennie M. Blackburn was recorded as living in the household of Finley Blackburn. Ancestry, http://ancestry.com; roll: M593, 395B, image: 2739, FHL film: 552705, National Archives microfilm, publication T132. Jennie's age in 1870 was recorded as four, suggesting a birth year of 1866. In the 1900 census, her birth date was recorded as July 1866, which correlated with the 1870 date.

55. Ohio Department of Health, amended birth record, vol. 2, 137, no. 2273 (1906), Sterling Joseph Glover, formerly "Joseph L. Glover"; Journal 17, 475, 28 March 1906, Green Township, Harrison County, probate court, Cadiz. In the 1910 census, his name was recorded as Joseph L. This author's father said he never wanted to be called "Joe," thus the reason he gave for changing his name to Sterling. Although he used the name Sterling starting sometime after 1910, he neglected to legalize it until 1967, which was necessary for a social security application. Also, Ohio Department of Health, Division of Vital Statistics, death certificate, vol. 36, section 2, 53–97 (1997), Sterling J. Glover; Harrison County Government Center, Cadiz. Sterling died on March 26, 1997, in Cadiz, Harrison County, Ohio, at the age of ninety.

56. Ohio Department of Health, delayed certificate of birth, no. 265888 (1912/1965), Faye Lida Grove; 8 November 1912, Jefferson County, Division of Vital Statistics, Columbus. Faye did not have a birth certificate until 1965. Also, Ohio Department of Health, certificate of death, 98–101 (1998) Faye L. Glover; Harrison County Government Center, Cadiz. Faye died on August 5, 1998, in Cadiz, Harrison County, Ohio; Harrison County, Ohio, marriage certificate no. 6521 (1933) Sterling J. Glover and Faye Grove; Harrison County Probate Court, Cadiz. Sterling and Faye were married on November 22, 1933.

57. Family Search, "Ohio, County Births, 1841–2003," https://familysearch.org, Jefferson, image 213, Elva Gosnell, 04 March 1878, county courthouses, Ohio. In the 1900 census, Elva's birthdate was given as May 1877, but since Elva was working as a domestic, someone else could have given the wrong information to the census taker. Also, Ancestry, "Ohio, Deaths, 1908–1932, 1938–2007," www.ancestry.com; Ohio Department of Health, Division of Vital Statistics, vol. 16157, Harrison County, certificate no. 36863, Elva Hastings, 26 May 1960, State Archives Series 3094, Ohio Historical Society, Columbus.

58. Family Search, "Ohio, County Births, 1841–2003," https://familysearch.org, Jefferson, image 132; Halleck H. Hastings, 02 Feb. 1884, county courthouses, Ohio; Family Search, "Ohio Deaths, 1908–1953," https://familysearch.org, image 1490, certificate of death, 79847, Halleck H. Hastings, 08 Dec. 1952, Ohio Department of Health; Jefferson County Marriages, marriage record book 17, 1902–1903, 224, certificate no. 26949, Halleck H. Hastings and Elva M. Gosnell, 04 Feb. 1903, probate court, Steubenville.

59. For information on Cora Gosnell's birth and death, see note 49.

60. Ohio Department of Health, certificate of live birth, vol. 6626, no. 94352 (18 June 1937), Division of Vital Statistics, Columbus.

61. Fort Wayne-Allen County, Indiana Department of Health, certificate of birth, book H-14, 115 (July 7, 1937), Larry Dean Goss; Indiana Board of Public Health, Fort Wayne, Allen County, Indiana; Ohio Department of Health and Vital Statistics, state file no. 2019092633, Larry Dean Goss, Cleveland, Cuyahoga, Ohio, died 30 Sept. 2019; Jefferson County, Ohio, marriage certificate no. 70262 (June 7, 1964), Larry D. Goss-Rena Lavon Glover, Jefferson County Probate Court, Steubenville.

62. 1900 U.S. census, Jefferson County, Ohio, Smithfield Township, population schedule, Enumeration District (ED) 72, 6484 (penned), dwelling 12, family 12, Addison McClain.

63. family 223, William L. Glover; Ancestry, http://www.ancestry.com, roll 1285, FHL microfilm 1241285, National Archives T623.

64. Family Search, "Ohio, County Births, 1841–2003," http://familysearch.org, Jefferson, image 112; Jefferson County Courthouse, Ohio, "Charles C. Gosnell, 1871 Nov. 23, James H. Gosnell, Mary Brown."

65. 1880 U.S. census, Jefferson County, Ohio, Smithfield Township, population schedule, Enumeration District (ED) 107, 28 (penned),

dwelling 142, family 142. Clara D. Gosnell, age six, was recorded as living in the household of James Gosnell; Ancestry, http://ancestry.com, FHF 1255037, National Archives microfilm, publication T9; Find a Grave, "Clara D. Gutshall, 1955; Burial, Massillon, Stark, Ohio, U.S.A., Rose Hill Memorial Park Cemetery; Record ID 119708049," http://findagrave.com. Clara Gutshall's memorial states her birth and death dates as, "b. Mar. 30, 1873, d. Apr. 26, 1955."

66. Ancestry, "Ohio, Wills and Probate Records, 1786–1998," http://www.ancestry.com, entry for James H. Gosnell, 4 Nov. 1899, Jefferson, citing Ohio County, District and Probate Courts.

67. 1900 U.S. census, Jefferson County, Ohio, Smithfield Township, population schedule, Enumeration District 72, 10 (penned), dwelling 203, family 203, Jeff Rainbow; Ancestry, http://www.ancestry.com, FHL microfilm 1241289.

68. Family Search, "Ohio Marriages, 1800–1958," https://familysearch.org, Jefferson Rainbow and Martha Norris, 05 Aug. 1884; Jefferson County, Ohio, reference 2:3KZKJ6L; FHL microfilm 900,071.

BIBLIOGRAPHY

This chronological list of articles (1–75) was taken from the following newspapers in Steubenville, Ohio: *Daily Gazette*, *Herald Star* and *Weekly Gazette*. The newspapers were accessed on Ancestry.com or viewed on newspaper microfilm at the Schiappa Library in Steubenville or the Puskarich Library in Cadiz.

1. *Steubenville* (OH) *Herald Star.* "Assassinated, Jas. H. Gosnell, a Farmer of Mt. Pleasant Tp." November 6, 1899, 8. Schiappa Library, newspaper microfilm, roll C-1.
2. *Herald Star.* "No Clue Has Been Found as to Who Shot Farmer Gosnell." November 7, 1899, 5. Schiappa Library, newspaper microfilm, roll C-1.
3. *Herald Star.* "Nothing New." November 8, 1899, 8. Schiappa Library, newspaper microfilm, roll C-1.
4. *Herald Star.* "No Clue Yet Discovered to the Assassin of James Gosnell." November 9, 1899, 8. Schiappa Library, newspaper microfilm, roll C-1.
5. *Herald Star.* "Snap Shots." November 13, 1899, 5. Shiappa Library, newspaper microfilm, roll C-1.
6. *Herald Star.* "The Gosnell Murder." November 16, 1899, 2. Schiappa Library, newspaper microfilm, roll C-1.
7. *Herald Star.* "Hunting New Clews [Clues]." November 21, 1899, 8. Schiappa Library, newspaper microfilm, roll C-1.
8. *Herald Star.* "Proposed Suicide." November 22, 1899, 5, column 3. Ancestry.com database. (Also, *Herald Star.* "Another Clue." November 22,

1899, 5, column 1. And, *Herald Star.* Short notice beginning "Prosecuting Attorney." November 22, 1899, 5.)

9. *Steubenville Daily Gazette.* "Much Levity." November 24, 1899, 5. https://puskarich.advantage-preservation.com/viewer.

10. *Steubenville Weekly Herald.* "The Gosnell Mystery." November 24, 1899, 1. Schiappa Library, newspaper microfilm, roll B-44.

11. *Herald Star.* "Held For Murder." November 24, 1899, 5. Schiappa Library, newspaper microfilm, roll C-1.

12. *Herald Star.* "Snap Shots." November 24, 1899, 2. Ancestry.com database.

13. *Herald Star.* "The Window in the Gosnell Residence through Which the Assassin Fired." November 29, 1899, 4 (drawing). Ancestry.com database.

14. *Herald Star.* "New Evidence Found." November 30, 1899, 8. Ancestry.com database.

15. *Herald Star.* "The Gosnell Case." December 8, 1899, 8. Citing the *Wheeling* (WV) *Register.* Ancestry.com database.

16. *Herald Star.* "The Missing Musket." January 8, 1900, 5. Ancestry.com database.

17. *Herald Star.* "First Degree." January 9, 1900, 5. Ancestry.com database.

18. *Herald Star.* "The Grand Jury." January 10, 1900, 5. Ancestry.com database.

19. *Herald Star.* "More Evidence in the Gosnell Murder Case." January 10, 1900, 4. Ancestry.com database.

20. *Herald Star.* "The Cramblett Case." January 11, 1900, 8. Ancestry.com database.

21. *Herald Star.* "Cramblett Arraigned and Counsel Appointed to Defend Him." January 16, 1900, 5. Ancestry.com database.

22. *Herald Star.* "$500 Reward." December 1, 1899, 3; December 18, 1899, 6; January 3, 1900, 6; January 4, 1900, 6; January 8, 1900, 3; January 9, 1900, 2; January 16, 1900, 2; and January 19, 1900, 3. Ancestry.com database.

23. *Herald Star.* "February Twelfth, the Day Set for Quincey [*sic*] Cramblett's Trial." January 17, 1900, 3. Ancestry.com database.

24. *Herald Star.* "The People." January 18, 1900, 5. Ancestry.com database.

25. *Herald Star.* "Cramblett's Relatives Held." January 19, 1900, 5. Ancestry.com database.

26. *Herald Star.* "The Cramblett Case." January 22, 1900, 5. Ancestry.com database.

27. *Herald Star.* "Affidavits in Cramblett Case." January 23, 1900, 5. Ancestry.com database.

28. *Herald Star.* "Mt. Pleasant." January 25, 1900, 3. Schiappa Library, newspaper microfilm, roll C-1.

29. *Herald Star.* "Postponement Probable." January 26, 1900, 5. Schiappa Library, newspaper microfilm, roll C-1.

30. *Herald Star.* "Cramblett's Money." January 30, 1900, 8. Schiappa Library, newspaper microfilm, roll C-1.

31. *Herald Star.* "Cramblett's Trial." February 26, 1900, 4. Ancestry.com database.

32. *Herald Star.* "The Cramblett Jury." March 12, 1900, 1. Ancestry.com database.

33. *Herald Star.* "Snap Shots." March 13, 1900, 5. Ancestry.com database.

34. *Herald Star.* "Snap Shots." March 22, 1900, 5. Ancestry.com database.

35. *Herald Star.* "Common Pleas Court." March 26, 1900, 5. Ancestry.com database.

36. *Herald Star.* "Cramblett on Trial for the Murder of James Gosnell." April 2, 1900, 5. Ancestry.com database. (In order to access April 2, 1900, it was necessary to click on March 2, 1900.)

37. *Herald Star.* "The Twelve Men Who Will Serve as Jurors in the Cramblett Case." April 3, 1900, 5. (Also, *Herald Star.* "Cramblett Trial Briefs." April 3, 1900, 1. Ancestry.com database.)

38. *Herald Star.* "Mingo." April 4, 1900, 2. Ancestry.com database. (Also, *Herald Star.* "A Love Story Woven into the Web of the Gosnell Tragedy." April 4, 1900, 8. Ancestry.com database.)

39. *Herald Star.* "The Threat Alleged to Have Been Made by Cramblett." April 5, 1900, 4. (Also, *Herald Star.* "Snap Shots." April 5, 1900, 1. Ancestry.com database.)

40. *Herald Star.* "State Rests." April 6, 1900, 5. Ancestry.com database.

41. *Herald Star.* "Guilty of Murder, the Verdict of the Jury in the Cramblett Case." April 9, 1900, 4. Ancestry.com database.

42. *Herald Star.* "New Trial Asked for in the Cramblett Murder Case." April 10, 1900, 5. Ancestry.com database.

43. *Herald Star.* "Snap Shots." April 12, 1900, 5. Ancestry.com database.

44. *Steubenville Weekly Gazette.* "Quincy Cramblett, Tried for His Life for the Murder of James H. Gosnell." April 13, 1900, 2. Schiappa Library, newspaper microfilm, roll B-46.

45. *Herald Star.* "Snap Shots." April 17, 1900, 5. Ancestry.com database.

46. *Herald Star.* "Cramblett Case, Motion for a New Trial Argued in Court." April 18, 1900, 5. Ancestry.com database.

47. *Herald Star.* "Snap Shots." April 30, 1900, 5. Ancestry.com database.

48. *Herald Star.* "Snap Shots." May 8, 1900, 5. Ancestry.com database.

49. *Herald Star.* "Snap Shots." May 11, 1900, 5. Ancestry.com database.

50. *Herald Star.* "The People." July 12, 1900, 5. Ancestry.com database.

51. *Herald Star.* "Cramblett's Attorneys Quit." September 27, 1900, 5. Ancestry.com database.

52. *Herald Star.* "Court Matters." September 28, 1900, 5. Ancestry.com database.

53. *Herald Star.* "Court Callings." October 1, 1900, 5. Ancestry.com database.

54. *Herald Star.* "Additional Cramblett Jurors." October 9, 1900, 5. Ancestry.com database.

55. *Herald Star.* "A Surprise Sprung in the Cramblett Murder Case." October 22, 1900, 5. Ancestry.com database.

56. *Herald Star.* "Briefly Told." October 23, 1900, 5. Ancestry.com database.

57. *Herald Star.* "More Jurors Secured in the Cramblett Murder Trial." October 24, 1900, 5. Ancestry.com database.

58. *Herald Star.* "Many Are Called but Few Are Chosen as Jurors in the Cramblett Trial." October 25, 1900, 5. Ancestry.com database.

59. *Herald Star.* "Jury Secured." October 26, 1900, 4. Ancestry.com database. Also viewed at Schiappa Library.

60. *Herald Star.* "Cramblett's Love Affairs." October 29, 1900, 5. Ancestry.com database.

61. *Herald Star.* "The Evidence." October 30, 1900, 5. Ancestry.com database.

62. *Herald Star.* "State Rests." October 31, 1900, 2. Ancestry.com database.

63. *Herald Star.* "Horse Tracks." November 1, 1900, 5. Ancestry.com database.

64. *Herald Star.* "Cramblett's Relatives Testify on His Behalf." November 2, 1900, 2. Ancestry.com database.

65. *Herald Star.* "The Jurymen." November 5, 1900, 4. Ancestry.com database.

66. *Herald Star.* "Moving Slowly." November 6, 1900, 2. (Also, *Herald Star.* "Briefly Told." November 6, 1900, 4. Ancestry.com database.)

67. *Herald Star.* "The Defense Rests Its Case." November 7, 1900, 2. Ancestry.com database.

68. *Herald Star.* "End in Sight." November 8, 1900, 8. Schiappa Library, newspaper microfilm, roll C-2.

69. *Steubenville Weekly Gazette.* "Cramblett, Case Closed and Lawyers Do Their Spouting." November 9, 1900, 4. Schiappa Library, newspaper microfilm, roll C-3.

70. *Herald Star.* "Charge of the Court." November 12, 1900, 3. (Also, *Herald Star.* "Cramblett Free." November 12, 1900, 8. Ancestry.com database.)

71. *Herald Star.* "Press Comment, What They Are Saying Regarding the Acquittal." November 13, 1900, 8. Ancestry.com database.

72. *Herald Star.* "Bloomfield." November 15, 1900, 2. (Also, *Herald Star.* "Richmond." November 15, 1900, 2. Ancestry.com database.)

73. *Herald Star.* "Press Comment." November 16, 1900, 2. Ancestry.com, database.

74. *Steubenville Weekly Gazette.* "Not Guilty Is the Verdict, and People Go Wild Over Cramblett." November 16, 1900, 5. Schiappa Library, newspaper microfilm, roll C-3.

75. *Steubenville Weekly Gazette.* "Cramblett Accused of Murder Similar to Charge Against Davis Drops into Town and Recalls Past." March 24, 1905, 6. Schiappa Library, newspaper microfilm, roll C-15.

76. Family Search. "Ohio, County Marriages, 1789–2013." http://familysearch.org.

77. 1910 U.S. census, Harrison County, Ohio, Green Township.

78. Ancestry. "Ohio, Birth Index, 1908–1964." http://www.ancestry.com.

79. Family Search. "Ohio, Deaths, 1908–1953." http://familysearch.org.

80. West Virginia Archives and History. "West Virginia Vital Records." http://www.wvculture.org/vrr.

81. Find a Grave. http://findagrave.com.

The following list of newspapers came from different cities in several states. Ohio and Pennsylvania newspapers covered the story on a regular basis. The list is likely not complete and may offer only a sampling of the varied locations where the story was followed. In Ohio, Cleveland and Cincinnati, some full-length articles were published, but more commonly, edited versions were published. Sources for this list: Newspapers.com, Genealogybank.com, Ancestry.com and the Puskarich Library in Cadiz, Ohio.

1. *Daily Intelligencer* (Wheeling, WV). "An Arrest Made." November 10, 1899, 4. Genealogybank.com

2. Cleveland (OH) *Plain Dealer.* "Applauded the Testimony." November 24, 1899, 1. Genealogybank.com.

3. *Cincinnati* (OH) *Enquirer.* "Obeyed Her Father's Desire." November 27, 1899, 2. Newspapers.com.

4. *Delphos* (OH) *Daily Herald.* "The Old Musket Found." January 10, 1900, 1. Ancestry.com database.

5. *Newark* (OH) *Daily Advocate.* "The Old Musket Found." January 10, 1900, 2. Ancestry.com database.

6. *Marietta* (OH) *Daily Leader.* "First Degree Trial Postponed." January 30, 1900, 1. Newspapers.com.

7. *Hillsboro* (OH) *News-Herald.* "First Degree Trial Postponed." February 1, 1900, 7. Newspapers.com.

8. *Pittsburgh* (PA) *Daily Post.* "Notes of Nearby Towns." April 3, 1900, 1. Newspapers.com.

9. *Pittsburgh* (PA) *Post-Gazette.* "Cramblett Not Particular." April 5, 1900, 4. Newspapers.com.

10. *Twin City News* (Uhrichsville, OH). "Quincy Cramblett Found Guilty." April 12, 1900, 5. Newspapers.com.

11. *Evening Review* (East Liverpool, OH). "A New Trial." May 5, 1900, 3. Newspapers.com.

12. *Idaho Falls* (ID) *Times.* "A Mysterious Deed." May 17, 1900, 4. GenealogyBank.com.

13. *Lead* (SD) *Daily Call.* "A Mysterious Deed." July 18, 1900, 7. Newspapers.com.

14. *Pittsburgh* (PA) *Post-Gazette.* "The Second Trial." October 22, 1900, 8. Newspapers.com.

15. *Denver* (CO) *Post.* "Cramblett Murder Trial." October 28, 1900, 17. GenealogyBank.com.

16. *Pittsburgh* (PA) *Post-Gazette.* "Shifting Crime on Another." November 3, 1900, 3. Newspapers.com.

17. *Independence* (KS) *Daily Reporter.* "A Mysterious Deed." November 10, 1900, 3. Newspapers.com.

18. *Pittsburgh* (PA) *Daily Post.* "Quincy Cramblett Was Acquitted." November 12, 1900, 9. Newspapers.com.

19. *Reynoldsville* (PA) *Star.* "Cramblett Acquitted." November 14, 1900, 6. Newspapers.com.

20. *Indiana* (PA) *Democrat.* "Cramblett Acquitted." November 14, 1900, 4. Ancestry.com database.

21. *Cadiz* (OH) *Republican.* "Cramblett Released." November 15, 1900, 4. Puskarich Library, newspaper microfilm.

ABOUT THE AUTHOR

Rena Glover Goss was born and grew up in Adena, Ohio. After graduating from Adena High School, she earned bachelor's and master's degrees in music education from Muskingum University and Indiana University, respectively. Rena taught music for twenty-seven years at public schools and universities in Ohio, Indiana and West Virginia. She served as a church musician for several years, played saxophone in a swing band and wrote articles for music publications.

Rena's other passions from a young age have been family and local history. She researched the maternal and paternal lines of her families in Jefferson County, Ohio, as well as the families of her husband, Larry Goss, who was from Fort Wayne, Allen County, Indiana, and wrote numerous articles about them for genealogical publications. She holds memberships in the Ohio Genealogical Society, Ohio History Connection, the Jefferson County and Harrison County Chapters of OGS, the Adena Historical Society, the Historical Society of Mt. Pleasant and the Smithfield Historical Society.

Visit us at
www.historypress.com